The Great North American Afghan is another in our series of afghans from the pages of *Knitter's Magazine* (issues 50–55). The designers were given no restrictions other than size of the square and its border. Their unique ideas will encourage you to build your knitting skills and learn new techniques.

Wonderful colors

CHOOSE to make it yours!

Choose the best **yarn**

Choose a **color** palette

12	20	4	21
9	13	15	8
10	23	16	14
6	1	5	17
19	7	11	24
22	18	2	3

Original Colorway

CASCADE YARNS **220**

100% Wool, 3.5oz (100g), 220yds (200m)

8010 Aran, 1208 Taupe, 8408 Rich Taupe, 8834 Pale Country Pink, 9424 Country Pink, 2401 Burgundy, and 9464B Sage Green

Choose your own arrangement of squares

Choose to **omit/repeat** one/several squares

Choose the **size** of afghan

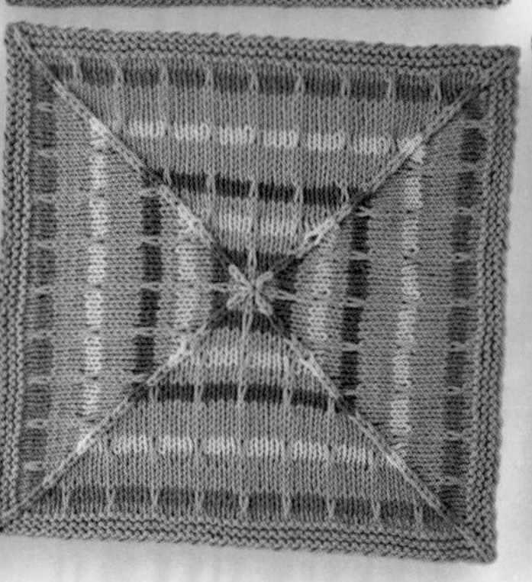

Play with a single square

We love this yarn and colorway for a summer throw. We chose Square 5, an easy one that highlights all the colors. Alternate the 2 cooler colors as backgrounds for a subtle checkerboard. For more color movement, work the remaining bands in a set order but start with each of the 5 colors.

CASCADE YARNS **Sierra**
80% Pima Cotton, 20% Wool;
3.5oz (100g); 191yds (175m)

(Paint can from bottom up)
404 Moss Tone, 55 Sunset, 410 Moth, 52 Sunshine, 431 Sprout, 06 Salmon, 07 Primrose, and 49 Pewter.

Limit your colors

You don't always need 7 colors. Rich browns and cream make this strong tonal statement. Short a color? Just repeat one.

CASCADE YARNS **Lana D' Oro**
50% Alpaca, 50% Wool;
3.5oz (100g); 219yds (200m)

(right to left)
1030 Ecru, 1057 Chocolate, 1085 Brown, 1051 Sienna, and 1040 Almond

Afghan finished measurements 48" x 60"

1	2	3	4
5	6	7	8
9	10	11	12
13	15	16	17
18	19	20	14

Square size 12" x 12"

Additional squares
21
22
23
24

Additional squares

Warm up on the easiest squares, and work your way up to the more challenging squares.

Getting started

1 Don't think of all of these squares as equals. Some are fairly simple, others a bit more challenging.

2 You don't need to make an exact copy of our afghan. Arrange the squares any way you like. You may choose to repeat several of your favorite squares, or build your afghan with just one pattern.

3 Adjust the number of squares to suit your project; a few more squares make a bedspread. One square makes an ideal pillow. Back it with a plain square or a second square.

4 Due to the nature of the various patterns, all squares may not block to an exact 12" square. When sewn together, small differences in size will ease into shape.

5 Unless otherwise noted, the gauge is 20 stitches and 26 rows to 4" stockinette stitch (knit on RS, purl on WS), using size 4.5mm/US7 needles. If a square has a different gauge or uses a different needle size, it will be noted. As always, the needle sizes listed are merely a starting point; choose the needle size that gives you the correct stockinette stitch gauge and adjust the others accordingly.

6 Most squares begin and end with 3 ridges (6 rows) of garter stitch (knit every row) and have a 3-stitch garter border at each side edge.

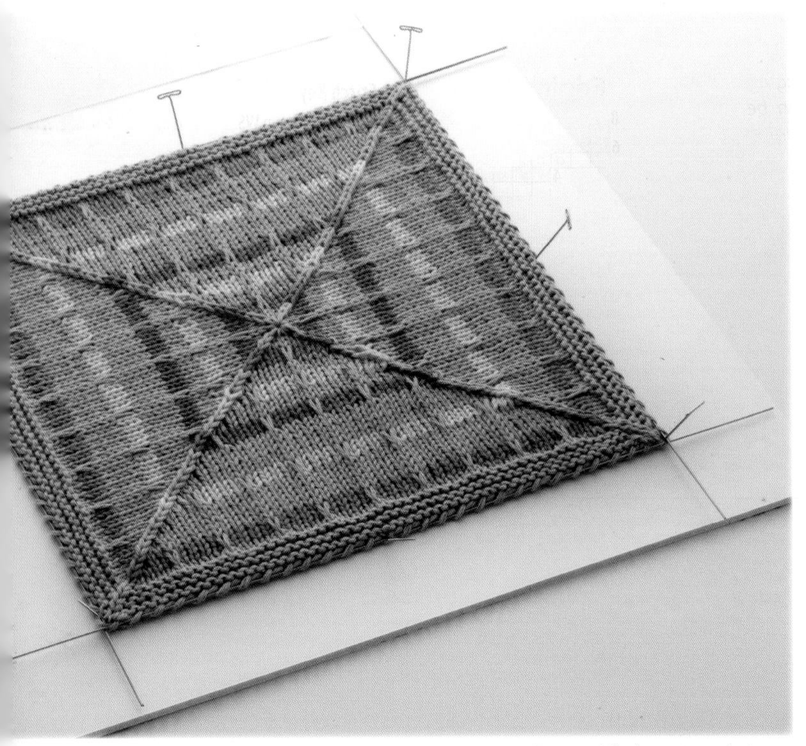

Be square! Blocking wires make it easy.

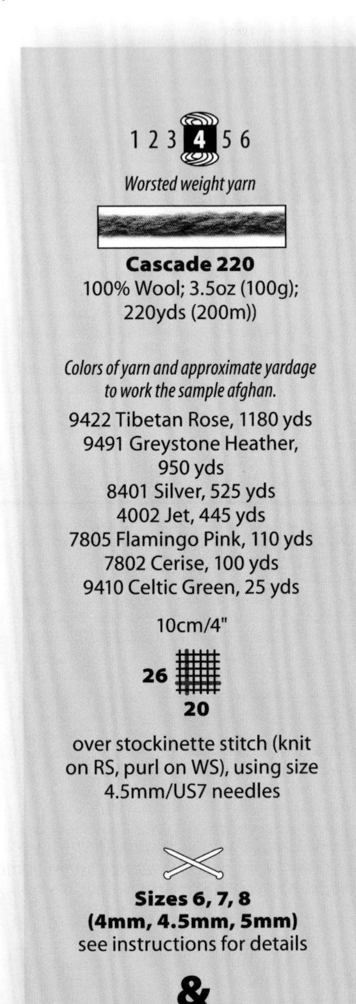

Care

An easy way to wash a large piece like an afghan in a top-loading washer is to fill washer with warm water, add Eucalan (a non-rinse wool wash), then afghan. Let soak as directed. Do not agitate or rinse. Skip directly to spin cycle. Lay flat to dry. (Floor covered with towels works well).

Finishing the afghan

Blocking the squares

Pin square to 12" and steam; never place the iron directly onto your knit piece. Or better yet, wash each square and pin out to dry. Then the squares will be clean and blocked.

Seaming the afghan

Sew squares together as shown in diagram, fudging a bit if necessary. Use a strand of the most prominent color of the 2 squares you are joining. We found it most successful to seam from the right side. Place pieces side by side, with right sides facing you. Thread blunt needle with yarn to match piece.

Edging

NOTE 1 *Edging is applied to afghan afterall squares have been sewn together.* **2** *Begin joining edging at seam between any 2 squares.* **3** *Edging can be worked separately then sewn to afghan. Or, edging can be applied to afghan as it is worked using a joining stitch (knit-on).*

Cast on 4 onto size 4.5mm/US7 needle.

Knit-on edging Work Edging Chart, attaching edging to afghan at end of every wrong-side row (Rows 2, 4, 6, 8). Pick up approximately 38 stitches along each square. Pick up at corners as follows: Work to within 2 stitches of corner stitch, ***[pick up 2 stitches in next stitch]** twice*, skip corner stitch; repeat from * to * once. Do not bind off; leave stitches on needle.

Sewn-on edging Work Edging Chart without joining stitch, working approximately 9½ repeats for each outside edge of each square. Do not bind off; leave stitches on hold. Seam straight edge of edging to afghan, easing in an extra repeat at each corner. Graft final open stitches to cast-on stitches (see page 25 for garter-stitch graft).

Seaming cast-on to bind-off

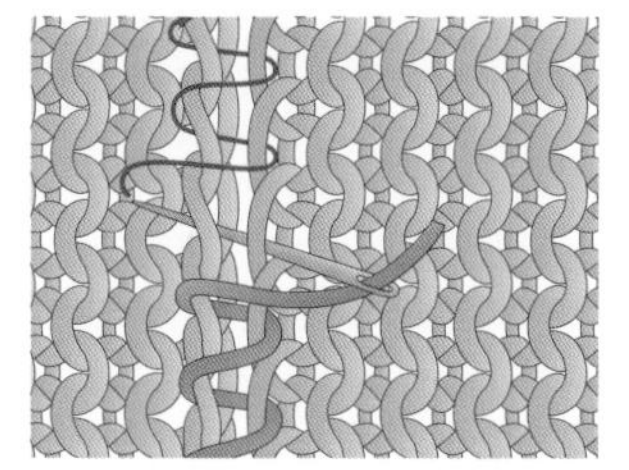

1 Pick up or catch a front leg of cast-on (right piece, above).

2 Cross to matching place on other piece and pick up or catch a front loop on bind-off (left piece, above).

3 Repeat steps 1 & 2 adjusting tension as you go.

Seaming garter edges

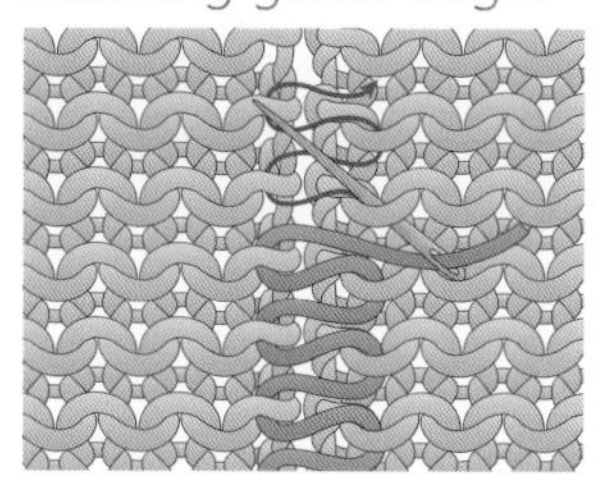

1 Pick up or catch a lower garter ridge from one piece (right piece, above).

2 Cross to matching place on other piece and pick up or catch an upper garter ridge (left piece, above).

3 Repeat Steps 1 & 2, adjusting tension as you go.

Edging Chart

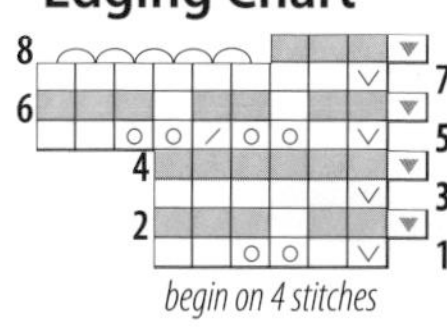

Stitch Key

- K on RS, p on WS
- K on WS
- Yarn over
- K2tog
- Sl st knitwise with yarn in back
- Join, work on knit-on edging only
- Bind off 1 st

IN OTHER WORDS

EDGING CHART *begin on 4 stitches*

Note *Slip stitches knitwise with yarn in back.*

Row 1 (RS) Sl 1, k1, **[yo]** twice, k2 — 6 stitches. 2 K3, p1, k2, join. 3 Sl 1, k5. 4 K6, join. 5 Sl 1, k1, **[yo]** twice, k2tog, **[yo]** twice, k2 — 9 stitches. 6 K3, **[p1, k2]** twice, join. 7 Sl 1, k8. 8 Bind off 5 stitches, k3, join — 4 sts. Repeat Rows 1-8.

1

Susan Guagliumi

CHESHIRE, CONNECTICUT

Twisted stitches are first cousins to 1/1 cables, but do not need a cable needle to hand knit; by machine they utilize a pair of two-prong transfer tools but not in the usual fashion. I work up a rhythm and find them very relaxing to knit; the end result always justifies the work! This design uses parallel columns of twisted stitches that cross and appear to interweave at the junction points because of the direction the stitches are twisted. I especially enjoy these patterns because they were some of the first handknit ones I brought to my machine years ago. I find that the longer I have been knitting, the less I differentiate between hand and machine knitting. After all, stitches are stitches and rows are rows whether you create them on a pair of sticks or a bed of metal hooks!

Note *See page 52 for unfamiliar abbreviations and techniques.*

Tibetan Rose
125 yds

4.5mm/US 7
or size to obtain gauge

MACHINE
Mid-gauge machine

Square

Handknit version

Cast on 60. Knit 5 rows, end with a WS row. Keeping first and last 3 stitches in garter stitch, work center 54 stitches in Chart pattern as follows: Work Rows 1–34 once, then Rows 3–33 once more. Knit 5 rows. Bind off.

Machine-knit version

MACHINE KNITTING ABBREVIATIONS

CO Cast on

COR (L) Carriage on right (left)

2RT Remove 2 stitches on 2-prong transfer tool. Insert a 2nd transfer tool from back to front through the same stitches, then remove the first tool. Rotate the tool one half turn to the left to return the stitches to needles.

2LT Work as for 2RT, but rotate the tool one half turn to the right to return the stitches to needles. Work as for handknit version with these notes for machine knitting: Begin with COR and do latch tool CO from left to right. Use garter bar to turn work over after each of the next 6 rows is knitted, ending COR after last turn. Knit 1 more row, then follow chart. Whenever COL, you should be twisting stitches; whenever COR, use latch tool to reform the 3 stitches at each edge as knit stitches to continue garter border. At end of chart, knit 1 plain row, then repeat garter rows using garter bar.

IN OTHER WORDS

1/1 RC (RT) Knit 2nd stitch on left needle in front of first stitch, then knit first stitch; slip both stitches off needle.

1/1 LC (LT) With right needle behind left needle, knit 2nd stitch on left needle through back loop, knit into front of first stitch; slip both stitches off needle.

Chart *over 54 stitches*

Row 1 (RS) K1, **[LT twice, k12]** 3 times, RT twice, k1. *2 and all WS rows* Purl. *3* K2, LT, **[LT, k10, RT twice]** 3 times, k2. *5* K3, **[LT twice, k8, RT twice]** 3 times, k3. *7* K4, **[LT twice, k6, RT twice, k2]** 3 times, k2. *9* K5, **[LT twice, k4, RT twice, k4]** 3 times, k1. *11* K6, **[LT twice, k2, RT twice, k6]** 3 times. *13* K7, **[LT twice, RT twice, k8]** 3 times, end last repeat k7. *15* K8, **[LT, RT twice, k10]** 3 times, end last repeat k8. *17* K9, **[LT twice, k12]** 3 times, end last repeat k9. *19* K8, **[RT twice, LT, k10]** 3 times, end last repeat k8. *21* K7, **[RT twice, LT twice, k8]** 3 times, end last repeat k7. *23* K6, **[RT twice, k2, LT twice, k6]** 3 times. *25* K5, **[RT twice, k4, LT twice, k4]** 3 times, k1. *27* K4, **[RT twice, k6, LT twice, k2]** 3 times, k2. *29* K3, **[RT twice, k8, LT twice]** 3 times, k3. *31* K2, **[RT twice, k10, LT]** 3 times, LT, k2. *33* K1, RT twice, **[k12, LT twice]** 3 times, k1. *34* Purl. Work Rows 3–33 once more.

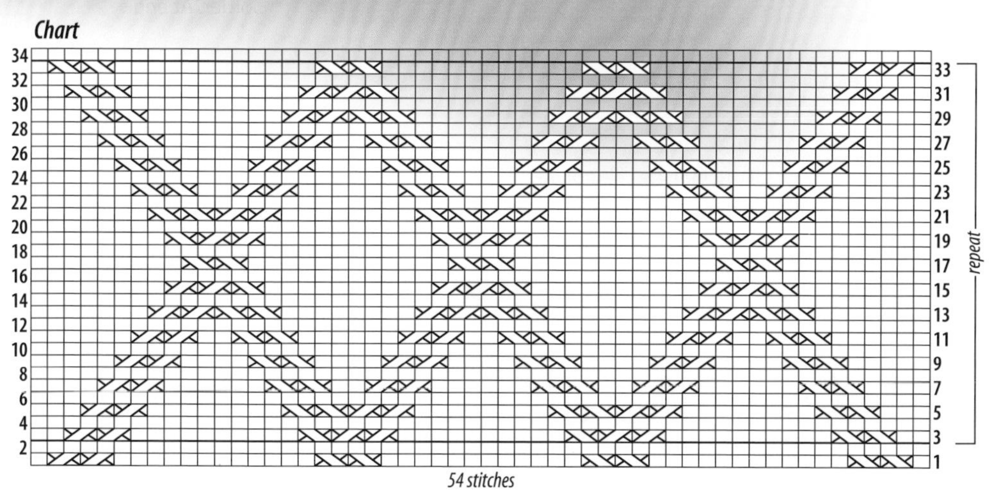

Stitch Key

- Knit on RS, purl on WS
- RT
- LT

2

Zabeth Loisel Weiner

STATEN ISLAND, NEW YORK

For my square I included some of my old favorites (traveling and twisted stitches, embroidery in tone on tone). As the square grew, I liked its flowery look. It made me think of a rose window with patterns evolving from patterns. The optional pinwheels, small on the sides and large at the center are my favorite types of embroidery. They look magical when complete (see page 5). Rose bobbles echo other squares and give this one a sense of belonging.

MC Silver
150 yds

CC Tibetan Rose
10 yds

4.5mm/US 7
16" (40 cm) long
or size to obtain gauge

5 **4.5mm/US 7**

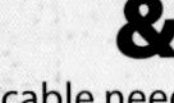

&
cable needle (cn)
blunt tapestry needle

Notes **1** *See page 52 for unfamiliar abbreviations and techniques.* **2** *Change to dpn when necessary.*

Square

With circular needle and MC, cast on 216. Join and work in rounds as follows: ***Begin Chart: Round 1*** **[Work chart over 54 stitches]** 4 times. Continue in pattern through Round 43—24 stitches. Cut yarn, leaving a 6" tail. Thread tail through remaining stitches and pull tight. Fasten off.

Finishing

Block square. With CC, work Herringbone stitch on stockinette stitch between Rows 7 and 9. With MC, work larger pinwheel at center of square, with spokes beginning at Round 41. Work 8 smaller pinwheels, follow chart for placement of center, with spokes approximately 5 stitches long.

IN OTHER WORDS

K1TBL K1 through back loop.

MAKE BOBBLE (MB) Knit into front, back, front of a stitch, turn, p3, turn, k3, turn, p3, turn, k3, pass 2nd and 3rd stitches over first stitch and off needle.

S2KP Slip last 2 stitches of repeat together knitwise, knit first stitch of next repeat, P2SSO.

S2PP Slip last 2 stitches of repeat together purlwise, purl first stitch of next repeat, P2SSO.

1/1 TWIST RPC Slip 1 to cn, hold to back, k1tbl; p1 from cn.

1/1 TWIST LPC Slip 1 to cn, hold to front, p1; k1tbl from cn.

1/2 TWIST LC Slip 2 to cn, hold to front, k1tbl; slip last stitch from cn to left needle and k1tbl; then k1tbl from cn.

2/1 RPC Slip 1 to cn, hold to back, k2; p1 from cn.

2/1 LPC Slip 2 to cn, hold to front, p1; k2 from cn.

2/1 TWIST RC Slip 1 to cn, hold to back, k2; k1tbl from cn.

2/1 TWIST LC Slip 2 to cn, hold to front, k1tbl; k2 from cn.

3/1 RIB RC Slip 1 to cn, hold to back, k1, p1, k1; p1 from cn.

3/1 RIB LC Slip 3 to cn, hold to front, p1; k1, p1, k1 from cn.

2/3 TWIST LC Slip 3 to cn, hold to front, k2; slip last stitch from cn to left needle and k1tbl; then k2 from cn.

2/3 TWIST LPC Slip 3 to cn, hold to front, k2tbl; slip last stitch from cn to left needle and p1; then k2tbl from cn.

2/3 LPC Slip 3 to cn, hold to front, k2; slip last stitch from cn to left needle and p1; then k2 from cn.

3/4 RIB LC Slip 4 to cn, hold to front, k1, p1, k1; slip last stitch from cn to left needle and p1; then k1, p1, k1 from cn.

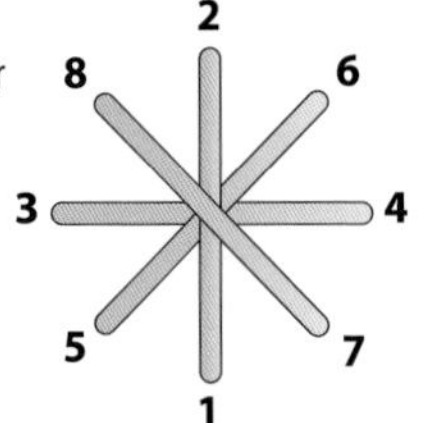

Pinwheel

Work spokes through square, bringing needle up to RS at odd numbers and down to WS at even numbers. Then keeping needle on RS of square, weave around spokes.

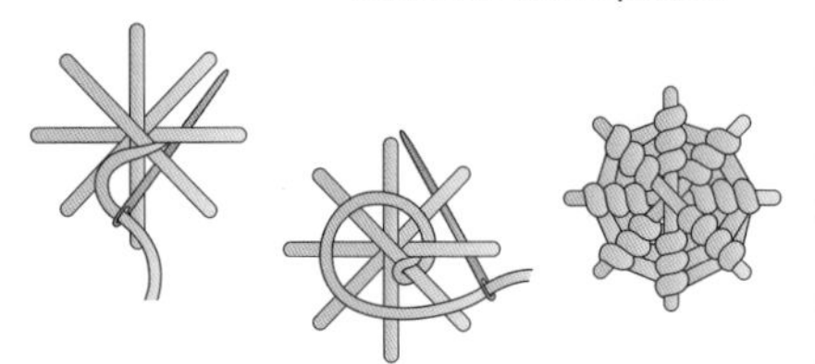

Herringbone stitch

Stitch Key
Knit
S2PP
Purl
S2KP
K1tbl
Center of small pinwheel
3/4 Rib LC
2/3 Twist LC
2/3 Twist LPC
2/3 LPC
3/1 Rib RC
3/1 Rib LC
2/1 RPC
2/1 LPC
2/1 Twist RC
2/1 Twist LC
1/2 Twist LC
1/1 Twist RPC
1/1 Twist LPC
Purl with CC
MB with CC
repeat

3

Stephanie Gildersleeve

MADERA, CALIFORNIA

The pattern in this square is special to me. It's interesting how designs evolve. Inspiration can come from many places. This pattern has two sources of inspiration. It is a variation on traditional diamond patterns from the British Isles. My favorites are those which include combinations of stockinette, reverse stockinette, seed or garter stitch, and lace. The resulting fabrics are non-curling and have a nice body to them, but are also lightweight. The patterns are quick to learn and are not boring to knit because you always seem to be beginning and ending a repeat at the same time.

A Christian Lacroix dress design with an orange full skirt quilted in a diamond pattern and accented with pompons inspired me to create this variation.

Tibetan Rose
150 yds

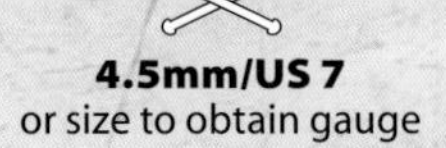

4.5mm/US 7
or size to obtain gauge

2 **4.5mm/US 7**

Note *See page 52 for unfamiliar abbreviations and techniques.*

Square

Cast on 55. Knit 5 rows, end with a RS row. Keeping first and last 3 stitches in garter stitch, work center 49 stitches in Chart pattern as follows: Work Rows 1–41 once, then work Rows 10-25 once more. Knit 3 rows. Work Rows 1–5. Knit 5 rows. Bind off.

IN OTHER WORDS

MAKE BOBBLE (MB) **[K1, (yo, k1) twice]** in a stitch, turn; **[slip 1, p4, turn; slip 1, k4, turn]** twice; slip 1, **[p2tog]** twice, turn; slip 1 knitwise, K2tog, PSSO.

Chart *over 49 stitches*

Rows 1 and 5 (WS) **[P2tog, yo]** to end, k1. *2, 3, 4, 6, 7, 8* Knit. *9* **[P2tog, yo]** twice, p41, **[yo, p2tog]** twice. *10* K4, **[k1, yo, SSK, k15, k2tog, yo]** twice, k5. *11* K4, **[p20, k1]** twice, k3. *12* K5, *k1, yo, SSK, k6, MB, k6, k2tog, yo, k1*, p1, repeat from *to* once, k5. *13* **[P2tog, yo]** twice, p1, **[k1, p8, slip 1, p8, k1, p1]** twice, **[yo, p2tog]** twice. *14* K4, **[k1, p1, k1, yo, SSK, k11, k2tog, yo, k1, p1]** twice, k5. *15* K4, p1, *p1, k1, p15, k1, p1*, k1, repeat from *to* once, p1, k4. *16* K5, *k1, p1, k1, yo, SSK, k4, MB, k4, k2tog, yo, k1, p1, k1*, p1, repeat from *to* once, k5. *17* **[P2tog, yo]** twice, **[(p1, k1) twice, p6, slip 1, p6, k1, p1, k1]** twice, p1, **[yo, p2tog]** twice. *18* K5, **[(p1, k1) twice, yo, SSK, k7, k2tog, yo, (k1, p1) twice, k1]** twice, k4. *19* K4, p1, ***[p1, k1]** twice, p11, **[k1, p1]** twice*, k1, repeat from *to* once, p1, k4. *20* K5, ***[k1, p1]** twice, k1, yo, SSK, k2, MB, k2, k2tog, yo, **[k1, p1]** twice, k1*, p1, repeat from *to* once, k5. *21* **[P2tog, yo]** twice, **[(p1, k1) 3 times, p4, slip 1, p4, (k1, p1) twice, k1]** twice, p1, **[yo, p2tog]** twice. *22* K4, **[(k1, p1) 3 times, k1, yo, SSK, k3, k2tog, yo, (k1, p1) 3 times]** twice, k5. *23* K4, p2, **[k1, p1]** 3 times, p6, **[k1, p1]** 7 times, p6, **[k1, p1]** 3 times, p1, k4. *24* K5, ***[k1, p1]** 3 times, k1, yo, SSK, k1, k2tog, yo, **[k1, p1]** 3 times, k1*, p1, repeat from *to* once, k5. *25* **[P2tog, yo]** twice, **[p1, k1]** 4 times, p5, **[k1, p1]** 8 times, p4, **[k1, p1]** 4 times, **[yo, p2tog]** twice. *26* **[K12, k2tog, yo, k1, yo, SSK, k3]** twice, k9. *27* K4, **[p10, k1, p9]** twice, p1, k4. *28* K5, *k6, k2tog, yo, k1, p1, k1, yo, SSK, k6*, MB, repeat from *to* once, k5. *29* **[P2tog, yo]** twice, p1, *p8, k1, p1, k1, p8*, slip 1, repeat from *to* once, p1, **[yo, p2tog]** twice. *30* **[K10, k2tog, yo, (k1, p1) twice, k1, yo, SSK, k1]** twice, k9. *31* K4, **[p8, (k1, p1) 3 times, p6]** twice, p1, k4. *32* K5, *k4, k2tog, yo, **[k1, p1]** 3 times, k1, yo, SSK, k4*, MB, repeat from *to* once, k5. *33* **[P2tog, yo]** twice, p1, *p6, **[k1, p1]** 4 times, p5*, slip 1, repeat from *to* once, p1, **[yo, p2tog]** twice. *34* K1, **[k7, k2tog, yo, (k1, p1) 4 times, k1, yo, SSK]** twice, k8. *35* K4, p1, **[p5, (k1, p1) 5 times, p5]** twice, k4. *36* K5, *k2, k2tog, yo, **[k1, p1]** 5 times, k1, yo, SSK, k2*, MB, repeat from *to* once, k5. *37* **[P2tog, yo]** twice, p1, *p4, **[k1, p1]** 6 times, p3*, slip 1, repeat from *to* once, p1, **[yo, p2tog]** twice. *38* K6, *k2tog, yo, **[k1, p1]** 6 times, k1, yo, SSK*, k3, repeat from *to* once, k6. *39* K4, **[p4, (k1, p1) 7 times, p2]** twice, p1, k4. *40* K5, *k2tog, yo, **[k1, p1]** 7 times, k1, yo, SSK*, k1, repeat from *to* once, k5. *41* **[P2tog, yo]** twice, **[p3, (k1, p1) 8 times, p1]** twice, p1, **[yo, p2tog]** twice.

Chart
49 stitches
Stitch Key
Knit on RS, purl on WS
Purl on RS, knit on WS
K2tog on RS, p2tog on WS
SSK
Yarn over
MB
Sl1 purlwise with yarn at WS of work

4

Pam Allen

CAMDEN, MAINE

My square is somewhat of a surprise. I had no idea that working slip-stitch in the round (or square) would create a crocheted granny-square look. One of the reasons I like to work with slip-stitch is that I find it hard to predict exactly what they will look like when knit. You can't chart a pattern in the same way that you can Fair Isle or intarsia. It's perfect for spontaneous, experimental knitting—you can forget planning and forethought. It's fairly mindless since you use only one color per row—no carrying yarns. And once you get the hang of it, the patterns often invent themselves. Another benefit of using slip-stitch is that it draws up, like garter stitch, making it possible to increase on every other round and get a piece that lies flat.

A Jet
B Greystone Heather
75 yds each

C Cerise
D Tibetan Rose
E Flamingo Pink
10 yds each

4.5mm/US 7
24" (60cm) long

5 **4.5mm/US 7**
or size to obtain gauge

Stitch markers

Notes

1 *See page 52 for unfamiliar abbreviations and techniques.* **2** *Repeat instructions for each dpn. Change to circular needle when necessary, placing markers between repeats.* **3** *Slip stitches purlwise with yarn in back.*

KOK K1, yo, k1 into corner stitch (2 stitches increased).
K1B K1 in row below stitch on left needle (see illustration).

Square

With A, cast on 8 using circle cast-on. Divide stitches evenly among 4 dpn. Join and work in rounds as follows: ***Round 1*** Work Round 1 of chart over 2 stitches for each dpn — 16 stitches. Continue in pattern through Round 51. With A, bind off purlwise.

Finishing

Block square. Pull tail from cast-on to tighten center, and secure.

Knit in row below (k1b)

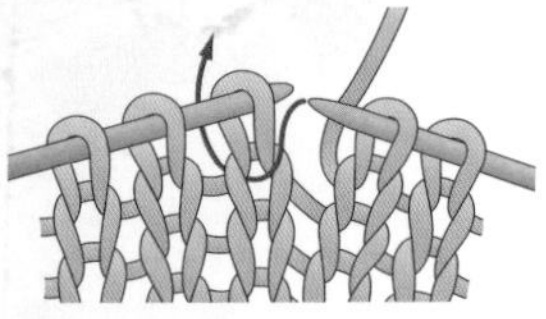

1 Instead of working into next stitch on left needle, work into stitch directly below it.

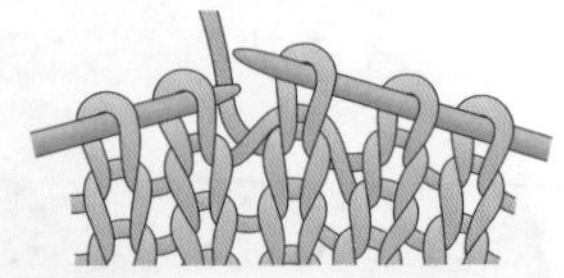

2 Pull stitch off left needle and let it drop.

Chart *begin on 2 stitches (each dpn)*

Round 1 With A, k1, KOK. ***2*** P2, k1, p1. ***3*** With B, k2, KOK, k1. ***4*** P3, k1, p2. ***5*** With C, sl 1, k1, sl 1, KOK, sl 1, k1. ***6*** Sl 1, k1, sl 1, k3, sl 1, k1. ***7*** K4, KOK, k3. ***8*** With A, k10. ***9*** P5, KOK, p4. ***10*** K12. ***11*** With B, sl 1, k3, sl 1, k1, KOK, k1, sl 1, k3. ***12*** Sl 1, p3, sl 1, p2, k1, p2, sl 1, p3. ***13*** With C, k2, sl 1, k3, sl 1, KOK, sl 1, k3, sl 1, k1. ***14*** K2, **[sl 1, k3]** 3 times, sl 1, k1. ***15*** K8, KOK, k7. ***16*** With D, **[sl 1, k3]** twice, sl 1, k1, **[sl 1, k3]** twice. ***17*** With B, **[sl 1, k3]** twice, sl 1, KOK, **[sl 1, k3]** twice. ***18*** K20. ***19*** K10, KOK, k9. ***20*** With E, **[sl 1, k1]** 11 times. ***21*** **[Sl 1, k1]** 5 times, sl 1, KOK, **[sl 1, k1]** 5 times. ***22*** With A, **[k1, sl 1]** 12 times. ***23*** K12, KOK, k11. ***24*** With C, **[sl 1, k3]** 3 times, sl 1, k1, **[sl 1, k3]** 3 times. ***25*** **[Sl 1, k3]** 3 times, sl 1, KOK, **[sl 1, k3]** 3 times. ***26*** With B, **[k1, sl 3]** 3 times, k5, **[sl 3, k1]** twice, sl 3. ***27*** K2, **[sl 1, k3]** 3 times, KOK, **[k3, sl 1]** 3 times, k1. ***28*** K2, **[p1, k3]** twice, p1, k9, **[p1, k3]** twice, p1, k1. ***29*** K15, KOK, k14. ***30*** K32. ***31*** With C, k16, KOK, k15. ***32*** P17, k1, p16. ***33*** With B, k17, KOK, k16. ***34*** P18, k1, p17. ***35*** K18, KOK, k17. ***36*** With D, k38. ***37*** With C, **[k1, k1b]** 9 times, k1, KOK, **[k1, k1b]** 9 times. ***38*** P20, k1, p19. ***39*** With E, **[k1b, k1]** 10 times, KOK, **[k1, k1b]** 9 times, k1. ***40*** P21, k1, p20. ***41*** With B, **[k1, k1b]** 10 times, k1, KOK, **[k1, k1b]** 10 times. ***42*** P22, k1, p21. ***43*** With C, **[k1b, k1]** 11 times, KOK, **[k1, k1b]** 10 times, k1. ***44*** P23, k1, p22. ***45*** With B, **[k1, k1b]** 11 times, k1, KOK, **[k1, k1b]** 11 times. ***46*** K48. ***47*** With A, k24, KOK, k23. ***48*** P25, k1, p24. ***49*** K25, KOK, k24. ***50*** P26, k1, p25. ***51*** K26, KOK, k25.

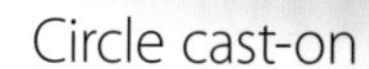

Circle cast-on

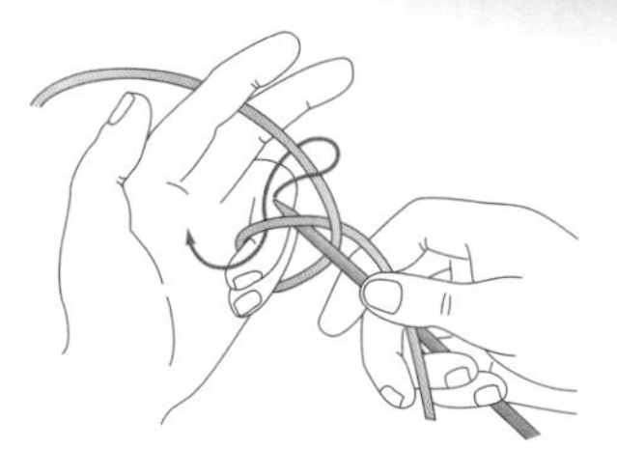

1 Holding tail in right hand and yarn in left hand, make a circle.
2 Insert double-pointed needle in circle and draw yarn through, forming a stitch on needle. Do not remove fingers from loop.

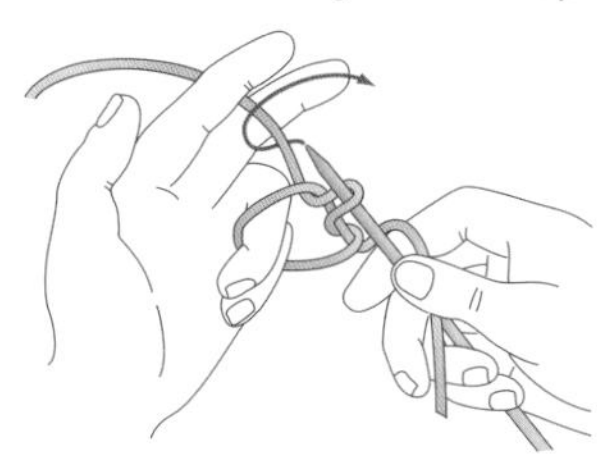

3 Bring needle under and then over the yarn, forming a yarn-over on needle.

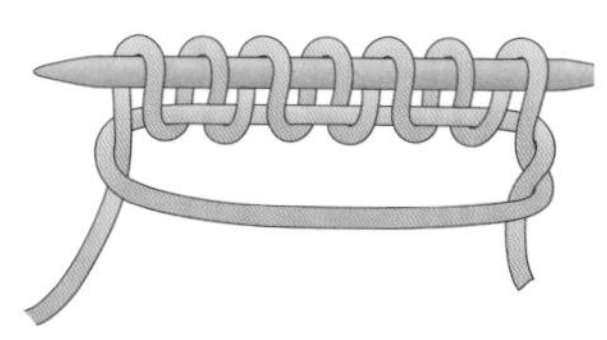

4 Repeat Steps 2 and 3, ending with Step 2. To cast on an even number, yarn over before beginning first round.
5 Arrange stitches on 3 or 4 double-pointed needles, pull tail slightly, then begin knitting around, working into the back loops of yarn-overs on the first round. Work several more rounds, then pull tail to close center.

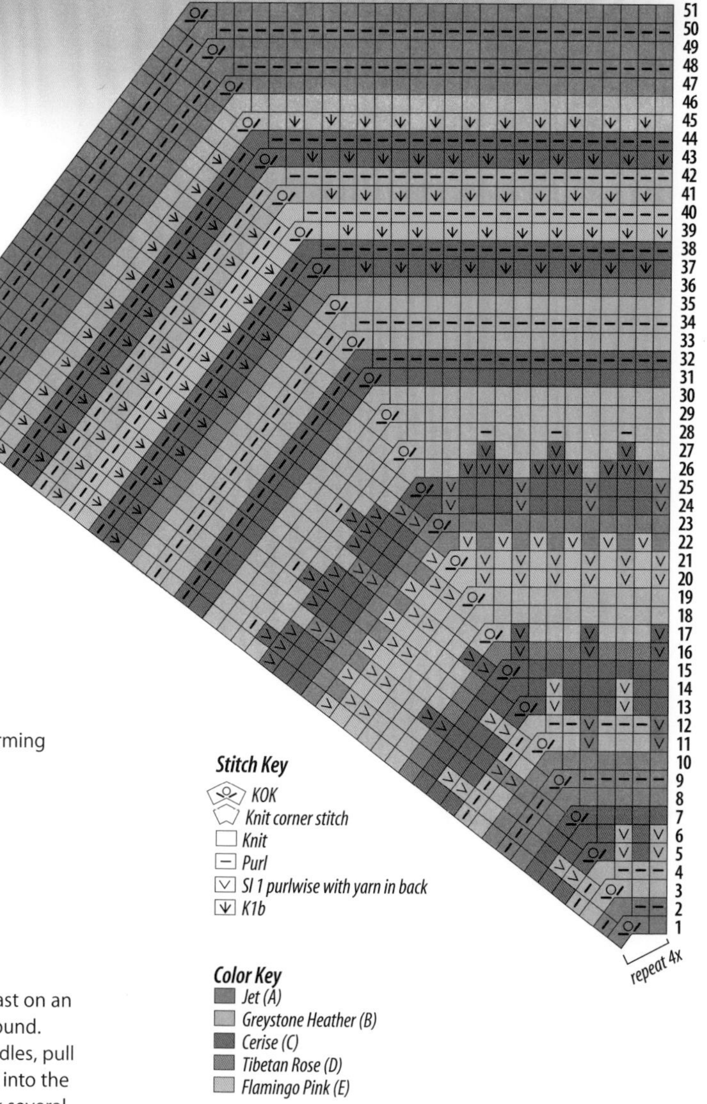

5

Elise Duvekot

HOCKESSIN, DELAWARE

Geometric designs tend to catch my eye wherever I go. My afghan square, titled "Fearless Symmetry," is certainly a reflection of that, since it is not merely symmetrical in terms of left and right, but rather it is the same on all four sides.

Notes **1** *See page 52 for unfamiliar abbreviations and techniques.* **2** *Change to dpn when necessary.*

Square

With circular needle and MC, cast on 224. Join and work in rounds as follows: *Round 1* **[Work Round 1 of chart over 56 stitches]** 4 times. Continue in pattern through Round 43—8 stitches. Cut yarn, leaving a 6" tail. Draw tail through remaining stitches and pull together tightly. Fasten off.

IN OTHER WORDS

S2KP2 Slip last 2 stitches of repeat together knitwise, knit first stitch of next repeat, P2SSO.

Chart *begin on 224 stitches*

Round 1 With MC, **[p55, k1]** 4 times. *2* K1, **[k53, S2KP2]** 4 times. *3* **[P53, k1]** 4 times. *4* K1, **[k51, S2KP2]** 4 times. *5* **[P51, k1]** 4 times. *6* K1, **[k49, S2KP2]** 4 times—200 stitches. *7* Knit. *8* With A, **[(k4, slip 1) 9 times, k5]** 4 times. *9* K1, **[k3, slip 1, (k4, slip 1) 8 times, k3, S2KP2]** 4 times. *10* K1, **[k2, slip 1, (k4, slip 1) 8 times, k2, S2KP2]** 4 times—184 stitches. *11* With MC, knit. *12* K1, **[k43, S2KP2]** 4 times. *13* K1, **[k41, S2KP2]** 4 times—168 stitches. *14* Knit. *15* K1, **[k39, S2KP2]** 4 times. *16* K1, **[k37, S2KP2]** 4 times. *17* With B, **[k3, slip 1, (k4, slip 1) 6 times, k4]** 4 times. *18* K1, **[k2, slip 1, (k4, slip 1) 6 times, k2, S2KP2]** 4 times. *19* K1, **[k1, slip 1, (k4, slip 1) 6 times, k1, S2KP2]** 4 times—136 stitches. *20* With MC, knit. *21* K1, **[k31, S2KP2]** 4 times. *22* K1, **[k29, S2KP2]** 4 times—120 stitches. *23* Knit. *24* K1, **[k27, S2KP2]** 4 times. *25* K1, **[k25, S2KP2]** 4 times. *26* With C, **[k2, slip 1, (k4, slip 1) 4 times, k3]** 4 times. *27* K1, **[k1, slip 1, (k4, slip 1) 4 times, k1, S2KP2]** 4 times. *28* K1, **[slip 1, (k4, slip 1) 4 times, S2KP2]** 4 times—88 stitches. *29* With MC, knit. *30* K1, **[k19, S2KP2]** 4 times. *31* K1, **[k17, S2KP2]** 4 times. *32* With D, **[k3, slip 1, (k4, slip 1) twice, k4]** 4 times. *33* K1, **[k2, slip 1, (k4, slip 1) twice, k2, S2KP2]** 4 times. *34* K1, **[k1, slip 1, (k4, slip 1) twice, k1, S2KP2]** 4 times—56 stitches. *35* With MC, knit. *36* K1, **[k11, S2KP2]** 4 times. *37* K1, **[k9, S2KP2]** 4 times. *38* With E, **[k4, slip 1, k5;]** 4 times. *39* K1, **[k3, slip 1, k3, S2KP2]** 4 times. *40* K1, **[k2, slip 1, k2, S2KP2]** 4 times—24 stitches. *41* With MC, knit. *42* K1, **[k3, S2KP2]** 4 times. *43* K1, **[k1, S2KP2]** 4 times—8 stitches.

MC Silver
125 yds

A Flamingo Pink
25 yds

B Greystone Heather
15 yds

C Tibetan Rose
D Jet
E Cerise
10 yds each

4.5mm/US 7
24" (60cm) and 16" (40cm) long
or size to obtain gauge

5 - **4.5mm/US 7**

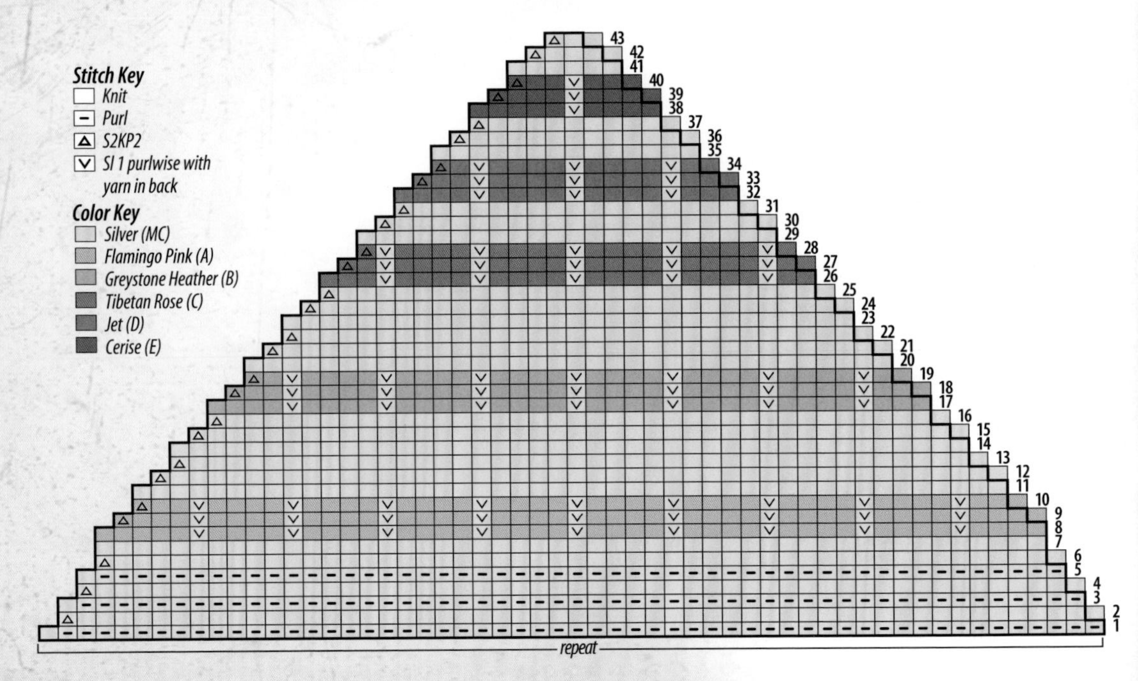

6

Gitta Shrade

TORONTO, ONTARIO

The basic idea for this square occurred to me when I was watching rain finding its way through the flowerbed in front of my window. By looking at something, I can see it in my mind in a different shape, texture, color combination, or proportion. It always translates into something usable for a design. I used traveling cables and I-cords to create this effective, but not difficult afghan square. To achieve an even more interesting piece, vary I-cord sewing positions on several squares.

MC Tibetan Rose
125 yds

CC Jet
25 yds

10cm/4"

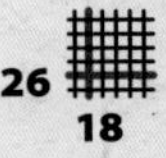

26 **18**

in stockinette stitch using larger needles (knit on RS, purl on WS)

5mm/US 8
or size to obtain gauge

4.5mm/US 7
24" (60 cm) long

2 **4.5mm/US 7**

Tapestry needle
Stitch holders

Note *See page 52 for unfamiliar abbreviations and techniques. See page 25 for pick-up and knit.*

INC 2 Knit into front, back, and front of next stitch.

Square

With larger needles and MC, cast on 58 using invisible cast-on. Work 69 rows of Chart. Place stitches on hold. With RS facing, circular needle and MC, pick up and knit 46 along left side edge, work across stitches of invisible cast-on as follows: Cast on 1, place 3 stitches of Cable 1 on hold, p9, place 3 stitches of Cable 2 on hold, cast on 1, p7, place 3 stitches of Cable 3 on hold, cast on 1, p8, place 3 stitches of Cable 3 on hold, cast on 1, p7, place 3 stitches of Cable 2 on hold, cast on 1, p9, place 3 stitches of Cable 1 on hold, cast on 1, pick up and knit 46 stitches along right side edge, work across stitches of Row 69 as for cast-on edge — 184 stitches. Join and work in rounds as follows: **Next round** **[P46, M1]** 4 times — 188 stitches. **Next round** With CC, **[k46, Inc 2]** 4 times — 196 stitches. Purl 1 round. **Next round** K47, Inc 2, **[k48, Inc 2]** 3 times, k1 — 204 stitches. Purl 1 round. **Next round** K48, Inc 2, **[k50, Inc 2]** 3 times, k2 — 212 stitches. Purl 1 round. Bind off all stitches knitwise with MC. Work Cables 1 as follows: Slip 3 stitches from holder to dpn. K3, knit into stitch below last stitch worked — 4 stitches. Work 4-stitch I-Cord for 6½". **Next row** **[K2tog]** twice. **Next row** K2tog. Fasten off. Work Cables 2 in same way, working I-cord for 1½". Work Cables 3 in same way, working I-cord for 1". With tapestry needle and MC, sew I-cords in position, using photo as guide. Steam gently without flattening.

I-cord

I-cord is a tiny tube of stockinette stitch, made with 2 double-pointed needles.

1. Cast on 3 (or more) stitches.

2. Knit 3 (or more). Do not turn work. Slide stitches to right end of needle.

Repeat Step 2 for desired length. The tube forms as the yarn is pulled across the back of each row.

Stitch Key

- Knit on RS, purl on WS
- Purl on RS, knit on WS
- 3/1 LPC: Sl 3 to cn, hold to front, p1, k3 from cn.
- 3/1 RPC: Sl 1 to cn, hold to back, k3, p1from cn.
- 3/2 LPC: Sl 3 to cn, hold to front, p2, k3 from cn.
- 3/2 RPC: Sl 2 to cn, hold to back, k3, p2 from cn.
- 3/3 LC: Sl 3 to cn, hold to front, k3, k3 from cn.
- 3/3 RC: Sl 3 to cn, hold to back, k3, k3 from cn.

7

A Silver
B Jet
50 yds each

C Greystone Heather
25 yds

D Tibetan Rose
10 yds

4.5mm/US 7
24" (60cm) long
or size to obtain gauge

4.5mm/US 7

Tapestry needle
4 split stitch markers

Sue Flanders

ROBBINSDALE, MINNESOTA

This square has a unique feature in that it uses 2-color knitting in the round, a very Norwegian technique, and still remains square. The decreases at the corners became part of the snowflake pattern which makes a very attractive design element. Traditional Norwegian sweaters have a main color, a contrasting color and a "touch of color" which is reflected in the color choices in this square.

Notes

1 *See page 52 for unfamiliar abbreviations and techniques.* **2** *End all rounds 1 stitch before beginning of following round.* **3** *Chart does not include 2 slip stitches of decreasing (knit stitch of decrease is first stitch of chart).* **4** *Change to dpn when necessary.*

Square

With circular needle and A, cast on 224. Join, being careful not to twist stitches. ***Round 1*** Purl to 1 stitch before end of round (see Note 2 above), placing marker in 1st, 57th, 113th and 169th stitches to mark corners. **2** Attach B, **[S2KP2, knit to 1 stitch before next marker]** around. **3** With B, purl. **4** With A, **[S2KP2, knit to 1 stitch before next marker]** around. **5** With A, purl. ***Begin Chart: Round 1*** With C, **[slip 2 stitches together knitwise, knit first stitch of chart, P2SSO, knit to last stitch of chart]** around. Continue in pattern through Round 25, working decrease at corner every round—8 stitches. Cut yarn leaving a 6" tail. With tapestry needle draw tail through remaining stitches twice. Pull snug and fasten off.

Finishing

Block square.

Color Key
- Light Gray (A)
- Dark Gray (B)
- Medium Gray (C
- Rose (D)

25
20
10
1

8

Michele Wyman

CHANDLER, ARIZONA

Whenever I start a new design, my vision is to create a project that only looks difficult (in other words, deceptively easy), has a classic look, and works up relatively quickly. My square is in keeping with that vision and has a bit of a Southwest flair.

MC Tibetan Rose
125 yds

A Greystone Heather
B Jet
10 yds each

10cm/4"

over Chart A

4mm/US 6
circular 16" (40cm) long
or size to obtain gauge

Note *See page 52 for unfamiliar abbreviations and techniques.*

TW2 Slip 1 purlwise with yarn in back, k1; pass slip stitch over knit stitch and leave it on left needle; knit slip stitch through back loop and drop from needle.

Square

With MC, cast on 61. Knit 5 rows. ****Begin Chart A: Row 1*** (RS) K3, **[TW2, p3]** 3 times, work 25 stitches of Chart A, **[p3, TW2]** 3 times, k3. **2** K3, **[p2, k3]** 3 times, work 25 stitches of Chart A, **[k3, p2]** 3 times, k3. Continue in patterns as established through Row 26. ****Begin Chart B: Row 1*** (RS) Work 18 stitches in pattern as established, work 25 stitches of Chart B, work in pattern to end. Work as established through Row 14. Work from * to * once. Knit 5 rows. Bind off.

Chart A

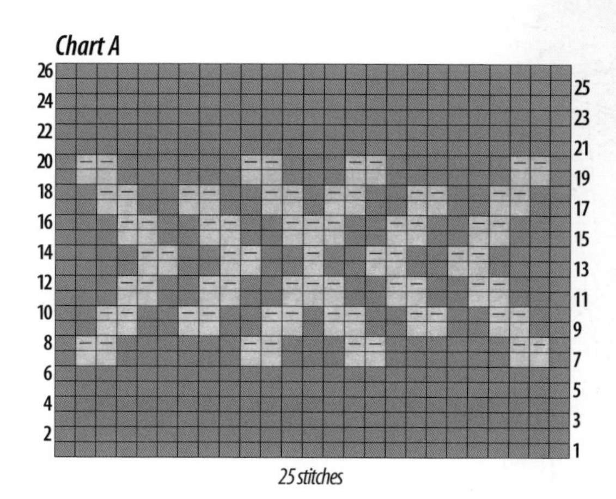

25 stitches

Chart B

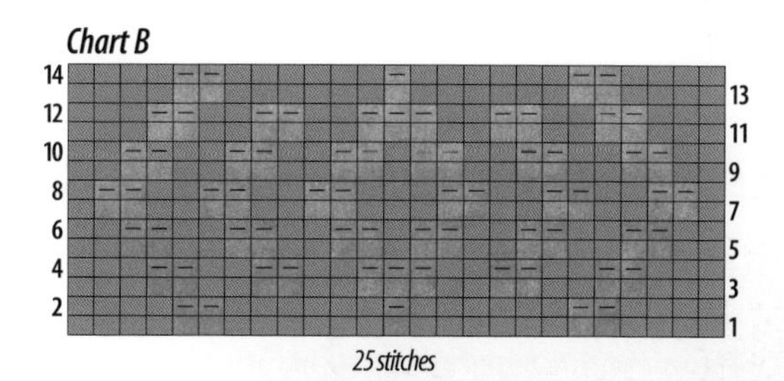

25 stitches

9

Charlotte Morris

LOS ALTOS, CALIFORNIA

My mother taught me to knit when I was 4 and we often sat knitting together, though my bright blue garter stitch squares weren't quite as well made as her sweaters. I like to use stitches in ways that take advantage of their intrinsic features, like the zigzag of the chevron that became the basis of the design for this square.

The border of my square is worked sideways in garter stitch which increases and decreases, forming a zigzag along the inner edge. Picking up stitches along the zigzags launches you straight into a stockinette stitch chevron with garter ridges, and a 3-needle bind-off allows the chevron to turn the corners. I kept the pinks in stockinette stitch dips between the garter ridges to add just a touch of color round the outside, widening towards the center like a starburst.

MC Greystone Heather
100 yds

A Flamingo Pink
B Tibetan Rose
50 yds each

10cm/4"

40 **19**

over garter stitch
(knit every row)

4.5mm/US 7
24" (60cm) long
or size to obtain gauge

5 **4.5mm/US 7**
or size to obtain gauge

Tapestry needle

Notes

See page 52 for unfamiliar abbreviations and techniques. **2** *When working Chart B, change to dpn when necessary.*

Square

BORDER

Side 1 With MC, cast on 9. Work Chart A as follows: work Rows 1–30 once, then repeat Rows 17–30 five more times. Work Rows 31–46.

Side 2 Work Rows 47-62 once, picking up stitches between garter ridges of rows below as indicated. Work Rows 17–30 six times, then work Rows 31-46 once.

Sides 3 and 4 Work as for Side 2. Fasten off. Sew corner seam.

Center

With RS facing, circular needle and MC, begin at corner seam (see Fig. 1) and **[pick up and knit (PUK) 5 to base of wave, (PUK4 along side of next wave, 1 stitch in top, 4 stitches to base) 5 times, then 5 stitches to corner, place marker — 55 stitches]** 4 more times — 220 stitches. Join and work circularly as follows: *Begin Chart B: Round 1* **[Work 55 stitches of Chart B]** 4 times. Continue in pattern through Round 9 — 188 stitches. *Round 10* Remove marker, turn right needle clockwise so that WS of work is facing outwards. Holding both needles in left hand with points facing in same direction, with dpn, use 3-needle bind-off to bind off 4 stitches (5 pairs of stitches used). Fasten off last stitch. Turn needle back to regular position. Replace marker. **[With MC, M1 at left edge of bind-off seam (see Fig. 2), work chart to 5 stitches before next marker, slip 5 stitches to right needle, remove marker, turn right needle as before. With a separate small length of MC and dpn, bind off 4 stitches, using 3-needle bind-off. Fasten off last stitch. Turn needle back to regular position. Continue with main yarn, M1 at right edge of bind-off seam, replace marker]** 3 times. Work chart to round marker, M1 at right edge of bind-off seam — 148 stitches. Work Rounds 11–19 — 116 stitches. *Round 20* Work as for Round 10, working chart as indicated for Round 20 — 76 stitches. Work Rounds 21–31 — 44 stitches. *Next round* Remove marker, turn right needle and bind off 3, using 3-needle bind-off. Fasten off last stitch. Return needle to regular position and replace marker, slip 3 stitches, **[slip 4 stitches, remove marker, turn needle and with a separate length of MC, bind off 3 stitches, using 3-needle bind-off. Fasten off last stitch. Turn needle, replace marker, slip 3 stitches]** 3 times — 12 stitches. *Next round* Removing markers as you go, with MC, **[insert left needle from back to front under strand at left of bind-off, knit strand together with next stitch, k1, slip next stitch knitwise to right needle, insert left needle from front to back under strand at right of bind-off, slip this strand knitwise to right needle, then insert left needle into these 2 stitches and complete SSK]** 4 times — 12 stitches. Cut yarn, leaving a 6" tail. With tapestry needle, draw tail through remaining stitches twice. Pull snug and fasten off.

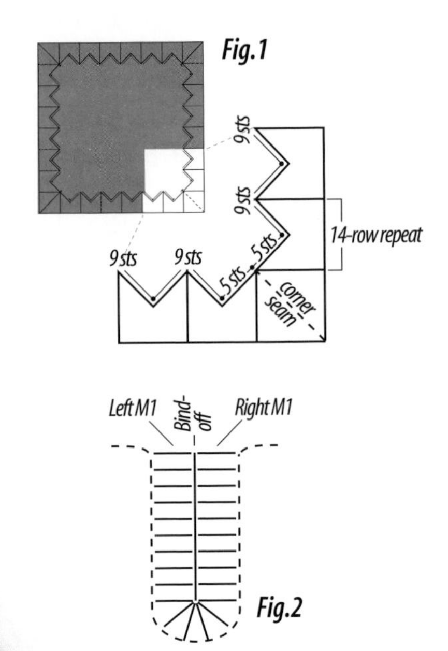

IN OTHER WORDS

WRAP STITCH AND TURN (W&T)
With yarn in front, slip 1 purlwise, bring yarn to back, slip stitch back to left needle, turn work, bring yarn to back.

Chart A *begin on 9 stitches*

Note Slip stitches purlwise with yarn in back unless indicated otherwise.

Row 1 K2, W&T. *2 and all WS rows (except 26, 28, 30)* Knit. *3* K3, W&T. *5* K4, W&T. *7* K3, sl 1, k1, W&T. *9* K3, sl 1, k2, W&T. *11* K3, sl 1, k3, W&T. *13* K3, sl 1, k4, W&T. *15* K3, sl 1, k5. *17* K3, sl 1, k3, k2tog. *19* K3, sl 1, k2, k2tog. *21* K3, sl 1, k1, k2tog. *23* K3, sl 1, k2. *25* K3, sl 1, k1, yo, k1. *26, 28, 30* K1, k1 through back loop, knit to end. *27* K3, sl 1, k2, yo, k1. *29* K3, sl 1, k3, yo, k1. *31–35* Repeat Rows 17–21. *37* K3, sl 1, k2tog. *39* K3, k2tog. *41* K2, k2tog. *43* K1, k2tog. *45* K2tog. *47* K1, pick up and knit (PUK) 1 from end of Row 45 (between garter ridges of Rows 44 and 46). *Note* On remaining RS rows, work to end of row, then PUK1 between garter ridges in rows below, as indicated. *49* K2, PUK1 at end of row 43. *51* K3, PUK1 at end of Row 41. *53* K3, sl 1, PUK1 at end of Row 39. 55 K3, sl 1, k1, PUK1 at end of Row 37. *57* K3, sl 1, k2, PUK1 at end of Row 35. *59* K3, sl 1, k3, PUK1 at end of Row 33. *61* K3, sl 1, k4, PUK1 at end of Row 31. *62* K9.

Chart B *55 to 11-stitch repeat*

INC 1 Knit into front and back of stitch.

Round 1 With MC, p55. *2* With A, k3, **[SSK, k2tog, k1, (inc 1) twice, k2]** 5 times, SSK, k2tog, k3. *3* With MC, k53. *4* K2, **[SSK, k2tog, k1, (inc 1) twice, k2]** 5 times, SSK, k2tog, k2. *5* P51. *6* With B, k1, **[SSK, k2tog, k1, (inc 1) twice, k2]** 5 times, SSK, k2tog, k1. *7* With MC, k49. *8* **[SSK, k2tog, k1, (inc 1) twice, k2]** 5 times, SSK, k2tog. *9* P47. *10* See Round 10 of center instructions, working chart as follows: k3, **[SSK, k2tog, k1, (inc 1) twice, k2]** 3 times, SSK, k2tog, k3. *11* P37. *12* With A, k3, **[SSK, k2tog, k1, (inc 1) twice, k2]** 3 times, SSK, k2tog, k3. *13* K35. *14* With MC, k2, **[SSK, k2tog, k1, (inc 1) twice, k2]** 3 times, SSK, k2tog, k2. *15* P33. *16* With B, k1, **[SSK, k2tog, k1, (inc 1) twice, k2]** 3 times, SSK, k2tog, k1. *17* K31. *18* With MC, **[SSK, k2tog, k1, (inc 1) twice, k2]** 3 times, SSK, k2tog. *19* P29. *20* See Round 20 of center instructions, working chart as follows: k3, SSK, k2tog, k1, **[inc 1]** twice, k2, SSK, k2tog, k3. *21* P19. *22* With A, k3, SSK, k2tog, k1, **[inc 1]** twice, k2, SSK, k2tog, k3. *23, 24* K17. *25* With MC, k2, SSK, k2tog, k1, **[inc 1]** twice, k2, SSK, k2tog, k2. *26* P15. *27* With B, k1, SSK, k2tog, k1, **[inc 1]** twice, k2, SSK, k2tog, k1. *28, 29* K13. *30* With MC, SSK, k2tog, k1, **[inc 1]** twice, k2, SSK, k2tog. *31* P11.

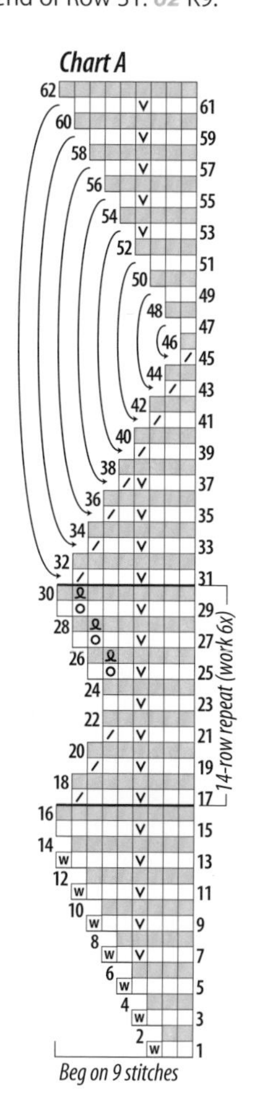

Chart A Stitch Key
- Knit on RS
- Knit on WS
- W & T
- Sl 1 purlwise with yarn in back
- K2tog
- Yarn over
- K1 through back loop
- Pick up and knit 1st between garter ridges of rows below, indicated by arrow

Chart B Stitch Key
- Knit
- Purl
- Knit into front and back of stitch
- K2tog
- SSK
- See Center instructions, Round 10
- See Center instructions, Round 20

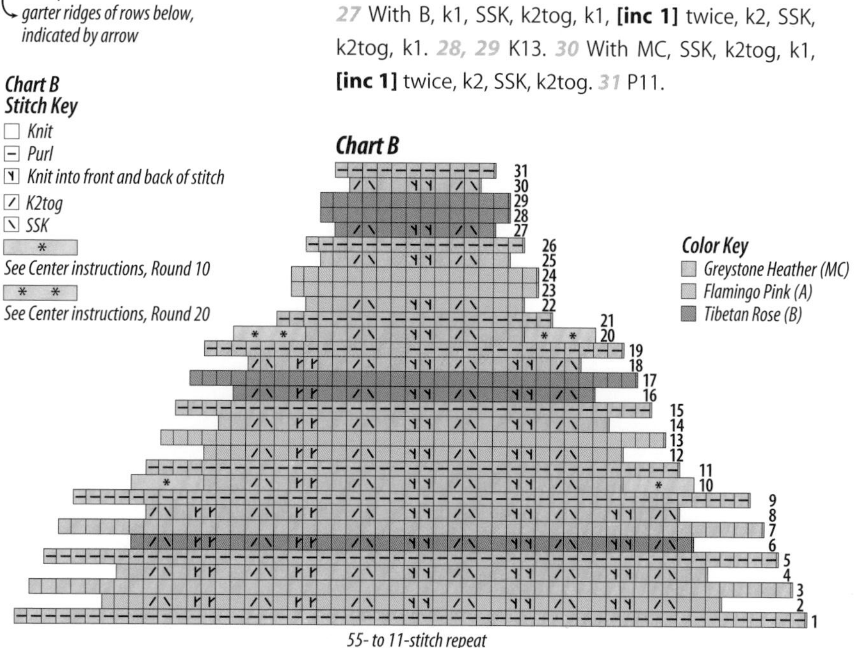

10

Debbie New

WATERLOO, ONTARIO

This knotted garter square tames a flowing band by confining it within bounds. It plays with the idea of a garter as a continuous closed ring. Wherever possible I have picked up rather than seamed and have used garter-stitch grafting and three different cast-ons for a uniform effect. You may want to weave in ends as you go as there are a number of color changes. The pattern of colors shown can, of course, be rearranged. A gradation from dark to light also gives a pleasing look. Garter-stitch grafting is used to complete the outer garter-stitch ridge while sewing together.

A Silver
B Greystone Heather
C Jet
50 yds each

10cm/4"
36
20
over garter stitch (knit every row)

4.5mm/US 7
24" (60cm) long
or size to obtain gauge

Stitch markers
Tapestry needle
Waste yarn

Notes **1** *See page 52 for unfamiliar abbreviations and techniques.* **2** *For ease in working, mark RS of square.*

Square

BORDER

With A, cast on 224. Do not join. ***Row 1*** (RS) **[K2tog, k52, SSK]** 4 times—216 stitches. ***2, 4*** (WS) Knit. ***3*** **[K2tog, k50, SSK]** 4 times—208 stitches. Cut yarn, leaving an 8" tail. With RS facing, slip 17 stitches to right needle. * ***Begin Center Triangle Chart: Row 1*** (RS) Join A and work Row 1 over 18 stitches. Turn work. Work Row 2 over 16 stitches—13 stitches. Continue in chart pattern through Row 14. Fasten off last stitch. With RS facing, slip next 8 stitches to right needle. ***Begin Corner Triangle Chart: Row 1*** (RS) Join A and work Row 1 over 18 stitches. Continue in chart pattern through Row 6. Cut yarn and pull through 2 remaining stitches. With RS facing, slip next 8 stitches to right needle. Repeat from * 3 more times, sewing mitered corner of border (being careful not to twist) before working last corner triangle.

COIL 1

With RS facing and C, leave an 18" tail for grafting later and begin at point AA of Coil 1 (see Coil Diagram), **pick up and knit (PUK) 14 evenly along left side of center triangle, k8, PUK14 along corner triangle, k8, PUK14 along right side of next center triangle, cast on 6, using loop cast-on—64 stitches. Turn work**. ***Next row*** K64, cast on 18, using invisible cast-on—82 stitches. ***Begin Coil Decrease Chart: Row 1*** (RS) With C, k10, **[place marker, work 12-st repeat]** 6 times. Continue in chart pattern, working repeat stitches between markers, through Row 21 (remove markers on last row)—16 stitches. Cut yarn, leaving a 15" tail. With WS facing and tapestry needle, thread tail through first 5 stitches, slip them off needle and pull together firmly. With RS facing, graft to garter edge, following diagram.

COIL 2

With RS facing and C, PUK18 evenly along top of Coil 1. Work between **'s of Coil 1—82 stitches. ***Next row*** Knit. Work Coil Decrease Chart and complete as for Coil 1.

COILS 3 AND 4

Work as for Coil 2, PUK18 along top of preceding coil.

Finishing

With RS facing, and open stitches at bottom, graft remaining garter edge to 18 invisible cast-on stitches, using garter stitch graft and 18" tail from beginning. Block square.

IN OTHER WORDS

Note Stitch count after bound-off stitches does not include stitches remaining on right needle.

Center triangle chart *begin on 18 stitches*

Row 1 Bind off 2, k15. ***2*** Bind off 2, k11, k2tog. ***3, 5, 7, 9*** K2tog, knit to last 2 stitches, SSK. ***4*** SSK, k7, k2tog. ***6, 8, 10, 12*** Knit. ***11*** K1, SSK. ***13*** K2tog. ***14*** K1.

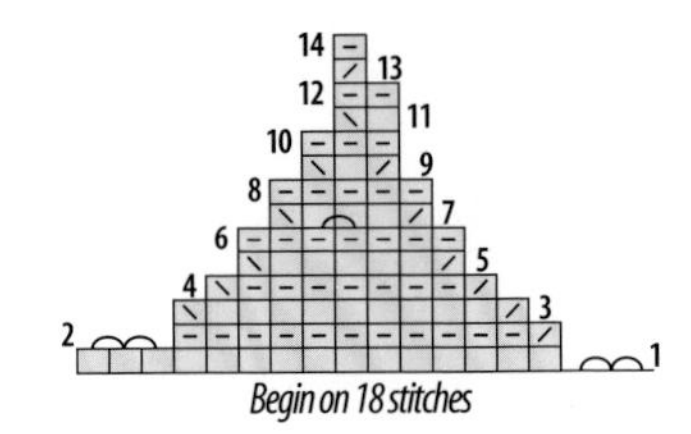

Corner triangle Chart *begin on 18 stitches*

Row 1 Bind off 1, k5, SSK, k2tog, k7. ***2, 4*** SSK, knit to last 2, k2tog. ***3*** K2tog, k2, SSK, k2tog, k3, SSK. ***5*** K1, SSK, k2tog, SSK. ***6*** K2tog, SSK.

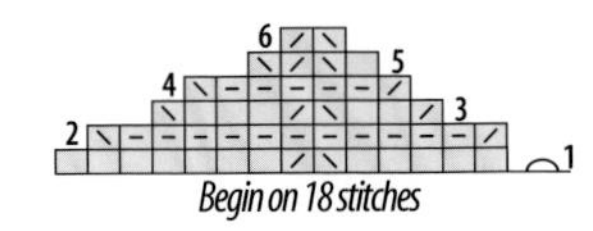

Coil decrease chart *begin on a multiple of 12 stitches, plus 10*

Row 1 With C, k10, **[k5, k2tog, k5]** to end. **2 and all WS rows** Knit with color of row below. **3** With C, k10, **[k3, k2tog, k6]** to end. **5** With B, k10, **[k5, k2tog, k3]** to end. **7** With B, k10, **[k1, k2tog, k6]** to end. **9** With A, k10, **[k5, k2tog, k1]** to end. **11** With A, k10, **[k2tog, k5]** to end. **13** With B, k10, **[k3, k2tog, k1]** to end. **15** With B, k10, **[k1, k2tog, k2]** to end. **17** With C, k10, **[k2, k2tog]** to end. **19** With C, k10, **[k2tog, k1]** to end. **21** With C, k10, **[k2tog]** to end.

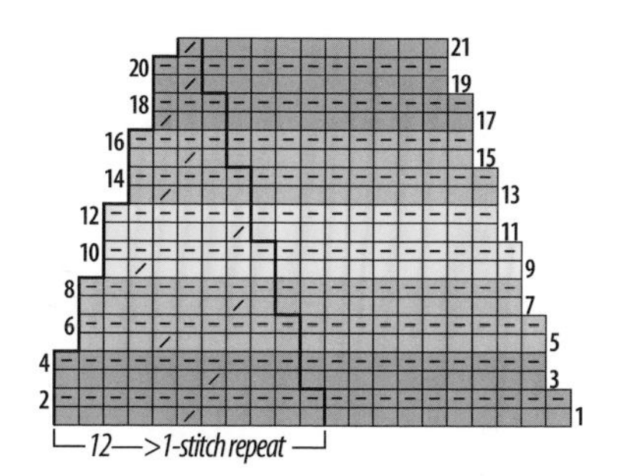

Stitch Key
- Knit on RS
- Knit on WS
- Bind off 1st
- K2tog
- SSK

Color Key
- Silver (A)
- Greystone Heather (B)
- Jet (C)

Coil Diagram

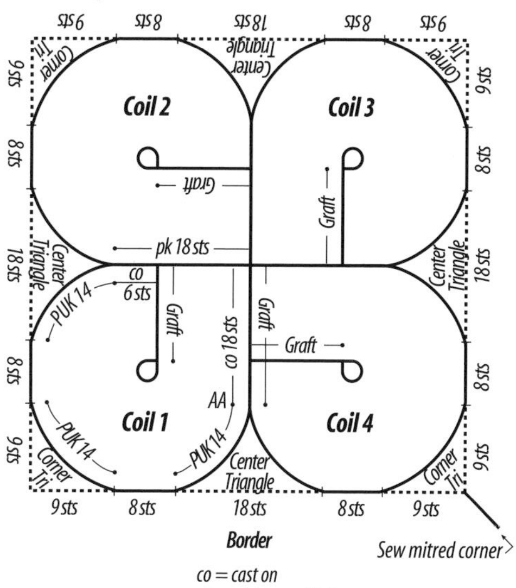

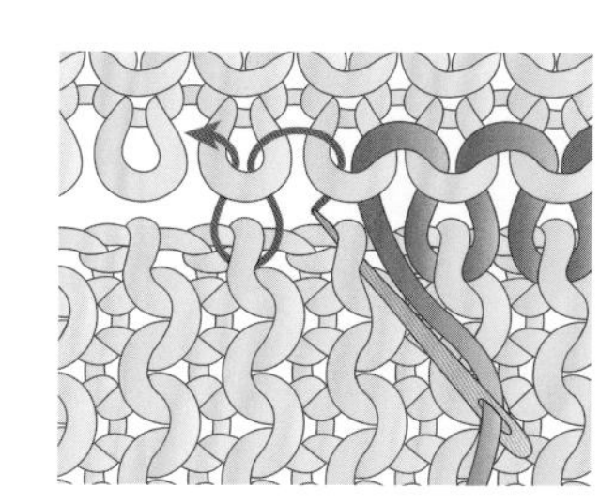

GARTER STITCH GRAFTING

Insert needle down into first stitch, *then under purl bump on garter edge. Bring needle up again into same stitch as before, then down into next stitch over; repeat from*.

11

Linda Cyr

CINCINNATI, OHIO

My square is an adaptation of a traditional quilt block called 'monkey wrench.' I confess to being a garter stitch snob — I've never liked it much, but after spending time tinkering around with it, I developed a new appreciation for this easiest of stitch patterns. I enjoyed working this square because once the numbers are figured out, it is pretty much mindless knitting and as the knitting spirals out from the center, there are very few ends to weave in when you are finished.

A Greystone Heather
B Jet
75 yds each

10cm/4"
40 / 20
over garter stitch (knit every row)

4.5mm/US7
or size to obtain gauge

Notes *See page 52 for unfamiliar abbreviations and techniques.* **2** *Follow diagram for placement of squares and triangles and color of triangles.* **3** *For ease in working, mark RS of Square 1.* **4** *Divide yarn into 2 balls of each color.*

IN OTHER WORDS

SK2P Slip 1 stitch knitwise, k2tog, pass the slip stitch over.

DEC 1 K2tog.

Square 1

With A, cast on 6. Knit 10 rows. ***Next row*** (RS) Bind off, do not cut yarn, do not fasten off. Place remaining loop on hold.

Square 2

With RS facing and B, pick up and knit 6 along right side of Square 1. Knit 9 rows. Bind off as for Square 1.

Square 3

With RS facing and separate ball of A, pick up and knit 6 along right side of Square 2. Complete as for Square 2.

Square 4

With separate ball of B, pick up and knit 6 along right side of Square 3. Complete as for Square 2.

Triangle 5

With RS facing, place last bound-off loop from Square 4 on needle and continuing with B, pick up and knit 10 along Squares 4 and 3 — 11 stitches. Knit every row and Dec 1 each side every RS row until 3 stitches remain. ***Next row*** SK2P. Do not cut yarn. Place remaining stitch on hold.

Triangles 6, 7, and 8

Using last bound-off loop from Squares 3, 2, and 1, work as for Triangle 5.

Triangles 9, 10, 11, and 12

Work as before, picking up 14 stitches in addition to bound-off loop.

Triangles 13, 14, 15, and 16

Work as before, picking up 20 stitches in addition to bound-off loop.

Triangles 17, 18, 19, and 20

Work as before, picking up 28 stitches in addition to bound-off loop.

Triangles 21, 22, 23, and 24

Work as before, picking up 40 stitches in addition to bound-off loop.

Finishing

Fasten off loop at end of each triangle. Sew seam to join Squares 1 and 4.

Pick up & knit

With right side facing and yarn in back, insert needle from front to back in center of edge stitch, catch yarn and knit a stitch.

12

Susan Levin

VENTURA, CALIFORNIA

Making and giving a Great North American Afghan is truly a labor of love—a love of knitting and love for the lucky recipient — so I designed the Heart of My Heart square. It is made with 2 of my favorite kinds of knitting: mosaic and cables. I designed mosaic hearts and complemented them with XO cables to represent hugs and kisses.

Since mosaic knitting is most effective when done in garter stitch, the gauge is very different than the stockinette cables. I compensated for the different gauges by using a short-row technique for the mosaic panel, so the center panel ends up with twice as many rows as the outer cable panels and border.

A Greystone Heather
125 yds

B Cerise
25 yds

10cm/4"

52 **18**
in Mosaic chart pattern

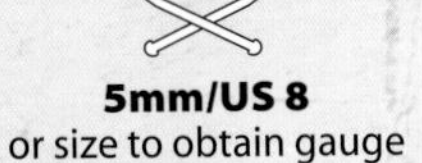

5mm/US 8
or size to obtain gauge

Cable needle (cn)
Stitch markers

Note *See page 52 for unfamiliar abbreviations and techniques.*

Square

With A, cast on 56. Knit 5 rows, decrease 1 stitch on last row — 55 stitches. ***Begin charts: Row 1*** (RS) With A, k3, place marker (pm), work Row 1 of Cable chart over 10 stitches, yarn back (yb), pm, join B, with yarn forward (yf), slip 1, yb (1 stitch wrapped), work Row 1 of Mosaic chart over 27 stitches, yf, slip 1, yb (1 stitch wrapped), pm. Turn work. **2** Yf, slip 1, work Row 2 of Mosaic Chart, yb, slip 1. Turn work. **3** With A, k1, work Row 3 of Mosaic chart over 27 stitches, k1, work Row 1 of Cable chart over 10 stitches, pm, k3. **4** With A, k3, Row 2 of Cable chart, k1, Row 4 of Mosaic chart, k1, Row 2 of Cable chart, k3. Continue as established, working 4 rows of Mosaic chart for every 2 rows of Cable chart and garter stitch border, and wrapping 1 stitch at each side of Mosaic chart every B row, through Row 128 of Mosaic chart. With A, knit 5 rows, increase 1 stitch on first row. Bind off 56 stitches.

IN OTHER WORDS

2/2 RC Slip 2 to cn and hold to back, k2; k2 from cn.
2/2 LC Slip 2 to cn and hold to front, k2; k2 from cn.

Cable chart *over 10 stitches*

Rows 1, 5, 9, and 13 (RS) P1, k8, p1. ***2 and all WS rows*** K1, p8, k1. ***3, 15*** P1, 2/2 RC, 2/2 LC, p1. ***7, 11*** P1, 2/2 LC, 2/2 RC, p1. ***16*** Repeat Row 2. Repeat Rows 1–16.

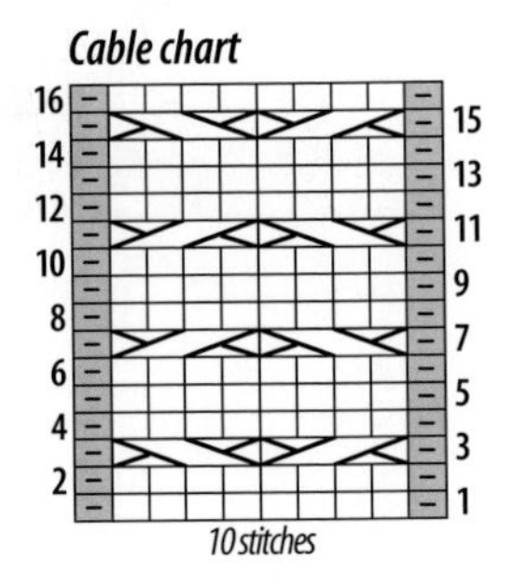

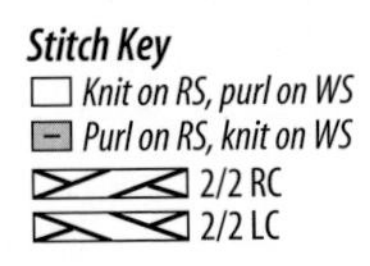

Mosaic chart

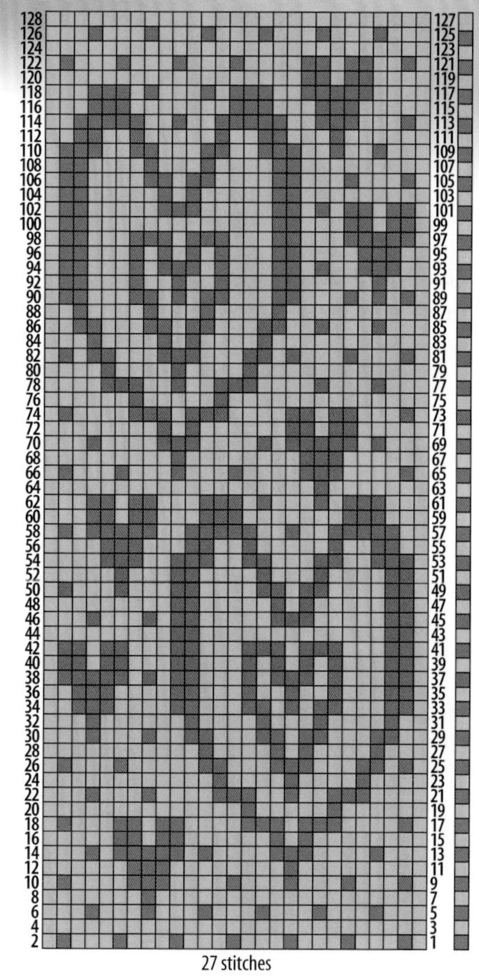

MOSAIC CHART NOTES

1 Each chart row consists of knit stitches and slip stitches (or just knit stitches). One color is worked each pair of rows. That color is shown in the column at the right of chart. **Rows 1 and 2** Work with B: Knit B stitches, slip A stitches purlwise with yarn at WS of work. **Rows 3 and 4** Knit all stitches with A. **Rows 5 and 6** Work with B: Knit B stitches, slip A stitches.

2 Work each chart row twice, once on RS; then on WS, knitting or slipping the same stitches.

3 Work 4 rows of Mosaic chart for every 2 rows of Cable chart. Wrap 1 stitch at each side of Mosaic chart on every B row to prevent holes (these stitches do not appear on chart).

Color Key

- *Greystone Heather (A)*
- *Cerise (B)*

13

Deborah Newton

PROVIDENCE, RHODE ISLAND

I like everything I design to have at least 3 elements — a traditional touch, an element of surprise, and something useful. I tried to use these notions in my afghan square. I've always loved ridged columns, often found in old Gansey sweaters. As an unexpected touch, I interrupted the columns with a totally unrelated pattern — reverse stockinette stitch with eyelets. And, since I always us my swatches to test something, I tried out a buttonhole at the center of my simple cable. In the future, I hope to place this buttonhole cable at the front of a cardigan!

Tibetan Rose
150 yds

10cm/4"

30  22

over Chart patterns

4.5mm/US 7
or size to obtain gauge

&

Cable needle (cn)

Note *See page 52 for unfamiliar abbreviations and techniques.*

Square

Cast on 55. Knit 5 rows, increase 9 stitches evenly across last (WS) row — 64 stitches. Knit 1 row. **Begin Charts A and B: Row 1** (WS) K3, then reading charts from left to right, **[work Chart A, Chart B]** 3 times, work Chart A, k3. **2** K3, then reading charts from right to left, **[work Chart A, Chart B]** 3 times, work Chart A, k3. Keeping first and last 3 stitches in garter stitch, work charts as established over center 58 stitches until 34 rows of Chart A have been worked twice, then work Rows 1–7 once more. **Next row** (RS) Knit and decrease 9 stitches evenly across — 55 stitches. Knit 5 rows. Bind off.

IN OTHER WORDS

3/3 LC Slip 3 to cn, hold to front, k3; k3 from cn.

Chart A

Rows 1, 3, 5, 7, 9, 11, 13, 15, 27, 29, 31, and 33 (WS) K2, p6, k2. **2, 6, 10, 14, 28, and 32** P2, k6, p2. **4, 8, 12, 16, 20, 22, 26, 30, and 34** P10. **17, 19, 23, and 25** K10. **18 and 24** P2, **[p2tog, yo]** 3 times, p2. **21** K2, **[k2tog, yo]** 3 times, k2.

Chart B

Rows 1, 3, 5, 7 (WS) P6. **2, 6, 10** K6. **4** 3/3 LC. **8** K1, SSK, yo twice, k2tog, k1. **9** P3, k1, p2.

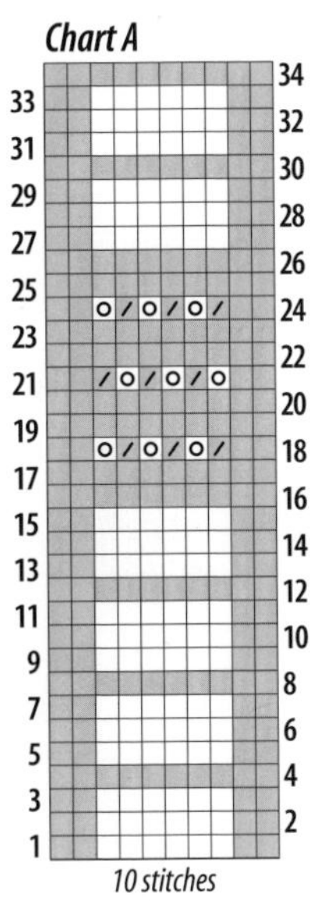

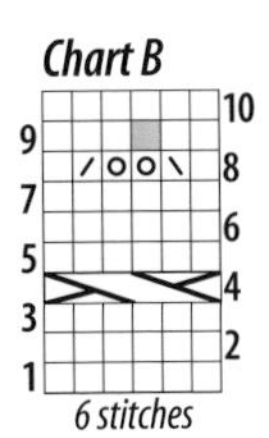

Stitch Key

- Knit on RS, purl on WS
- Purl on RS, knit on WS
- K2tog
- P2tog on RS, k2tog on WS
- SSK
- Yo
- 3/3 LC

14

Jean Frost

SAN DIEGO, CALIFORNIA

This square is based on a coverlet made by a Danish woman. I've never seen I-cord used in this way and was fascinated by the original article which appears to have been worked in one piece. Much patience went into producing such a coverlet.

Tibetan Rose
150 yds

4.5mm/US 7
or size to obtain gauge

2 **4.5mm/US 7**

Note *See page 52 for unfamiliar abbreviations and techniques.*

Square

Cast on 56 stitches. Knit 5 rows, end with a WS row. Keeping first and last 3 stitches in garter stitch, work center 50 stitches in chart pattern through Row 64. Knit 5 rows. Bind off.

IN OTHER WORDS

2-STITCH I-CORD (2IC) **[With dpn, k2, do not turn, slide stitches to other end of dpn]** 6 times. Slip stitches to right needle.

CHART *over 50 stitches*

Rows 1 and 5 (RS) **[P2, k2]**, end p2. ***2 and all WS rows*** Knit the knit stitches and purl the purl stitches. ***3, 7*** **[K2, p2]**, end k2. ***9*** P2, k2, p2, k38, p2, k2, p2. ***11, 15, 19, 23, 27, 31, 35, 39, 43, 47, 51, 55*** K2, p2, k42, p2, k2. ***13, 53*** P2, k2, p2, k18, 2IC, k18, p2, k2, p2. ***17, 49*** P2, k2, p2, k15, **[2IC, k1]** 3 times, k14, p2, k2, p2. ***21, 45*** P2, k2, p2, k12, **[2IC, k1]** 5 times, k11, p2, k2, p2. ***25, 41*** P2, k2, p2, k9, **[2IC, k1]** 7 times, k8, p2, k2, p2. ***29, 37*** P2, k2, p2, k6, **[2IC, k1]** 9 times, k5, p2, k2, p2. ***33*** **[P2, k2]** twice, k1, **[2IC, k1]** 11 times, **[k2, p2]** twice. ***57–64*** Repeat Rows 1–8.

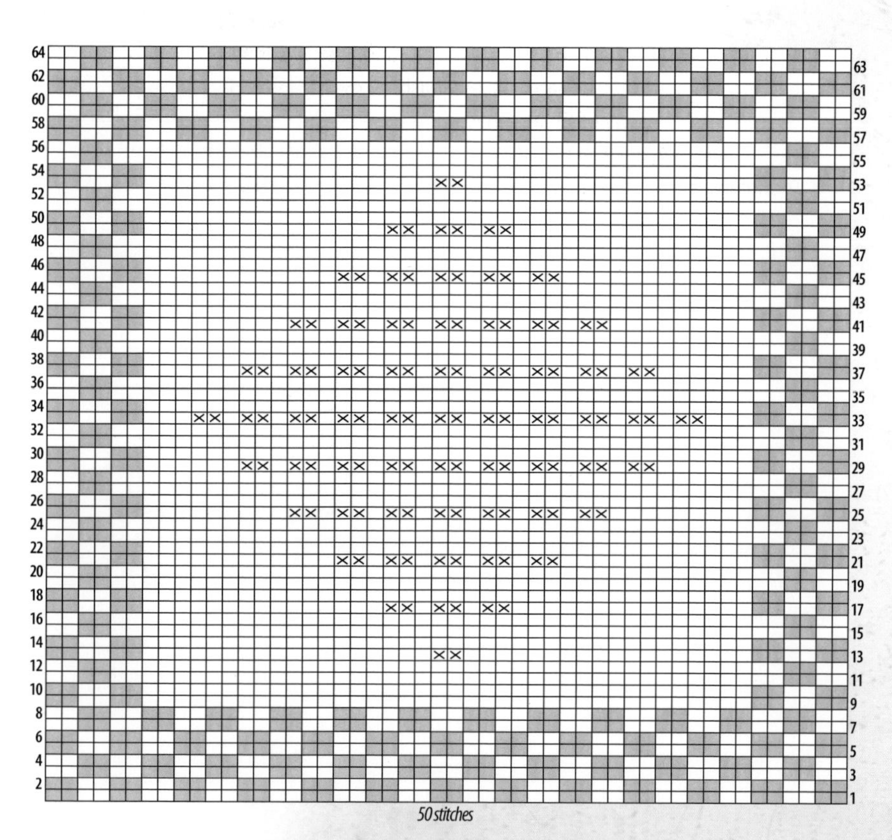

Stitch Key
Knit on RS, purl on WS
Knit on WS, purl on RS
2-st I-cord

15

Rick Mondragon

ALBUQUERQUE, NEW MEXICO

I like classic, wearable silhouettes with creative, unusual, or unexpected elements that make the look interesting and contemporary. My square follows this thinking: Pin stripes in 4 directions are surrounded and bisected with garter-ridge stripes. It is visually complicated but easily achieved. Circular knitting features a simple cast-on and easy and balanced increases (also mindless). The square could evolve into a fine upside-down raglan. Fold the square in half for a preview. The chart and printed words seem intense, yet after 10 quick rounds you'll have experienced all the techniques presented.

A Greystone Heather
B Jet
75 yds each

10cm/4"
30 / 20
over chart patterns

4.5mm/US 7
16" (40cm) long
24" (60cm) long (optional)

5 **4.5mm/US 7**
double-pointed needles (dpn) or size to obtain gauge

Notes

1 *See page 52 for unfamiliar abbreviations and techniques.* **2** *Take care to hold yarn in a consistent manner throughout.* **3** *Change to circular needles when necessary.*

Square

With A, cast on 16 using slip knot circular cast-on. Divide stitches evenly among 4 dpn. Join and work in rounds as follows: *Round 1* **[Work Round 1 of chart over 4 stitches]** for each dpn. Mark beginning of round. Continue in pattern through Round 45. With A, bind off all stitches purlwise.

Finishing

Block square (it may take some coaxing to lie flat and achieve a 12" square). Pull tail from cast-on to tighten center, and secure.

IN OTHER WORDS

KOK K1, yo, k1 into corner stitch (2 stitches increased).

Chart *begin on 4 stitches*

Note Repeat instructions for each dpn.
Round 1 With A, KOK, k3. *2* With A, purl. *3* With B, k1, KOK, k4. *4* With B, purl. *5* K1A, k1B, KOK with A, **[k1B, k1A]** twice, k1B. *6, 8, 10, 12, 14, 16* **[K1A, k1B]** across dpn. *7* K1A, k1B, k1A, KOK with B, **[k1A, k1B]** 3 times. *9* **[K1A, k1B]** twice, KOK with A, **[k1B, k1A]** 3 times, k1B. *11* **[K1A, k1B]** twice, k1A, KOK with B, **[k1A, k1B]** 4 times. *13* **[K1A, k1B]** 3 times, KOK with A, **[k1B, k1A]** 4 times, k1B. *15* **[K1A, k1B]** 3 times, k1A, KOK with B, **[k1A, k1B]** 5 times. *17* With B, k8, KOK, k11. *18* With B, purl. *19* With A, k9, KOK, k12. *20* With A, purl. *21* With B, k10, KOK, k13. *22* With B, purl. *23* **[K1 A, k1B]** 5 times, k1A, KOK with B, **[k1A, k1B]** 7 times. *24, 26* ***[K1A, k1B]**; across dpn. *25* **[K1A, k1B]** 6 times, KOK with A, **[k1B, k1A]** 6 times, k3B. *27* K2B, **[k1A, k1B]** 5 times, k1A, KOK with B, **[k1A, k1B]** 6 times, k1B, k3A. *28* **[K1A, k1B]** 14 times, k4A. *29* K2A, k2B, **[k1A, k1B]** 5 times, KOK with A, **[k1B, k1A]** 5 times, k2B, k3A, k1B, k1A. *30* K3A, **[k1B, k1A]** 13 times, k2A, k3B. *31* K2A, k2B, **[k1A, k1B]** 5 times, k1A, KOK with B, **[k1A, k1B]** 6 times, k1B, k3A, k1B, k1A. *32* **[K1A, k1B]** 16 times, k4A. *33* K2B, **[k1A, k1B]** 7 times, KOK with A, **[k1B, k1A]** 7 times, k2B, k3A. *34, 36, 38, 40* **[K1A, k1B]** across dpn. *35* **[K1A, k1B]** 8 times, k1A, KOK with B, **[k1A, k1B]** 9 times, k2B. *37* **[K1A, k1B]** 9 times, KOK with A, **[k1B, k1A]** 10 times, k1B. *39* **[K1A, k1B]** 9 times, k1A, KOK with B, **[k1A, k1B]** 11 times. *41* With A, k20, KOK, k23. *42* With A, purl. *43* With B, k21, KOK, k24. *44* With B, purl. *45* With A, k22, KOK, k25.

SLIP KNOT CIRCULAR CAST-ON

an even number of stitches.

Make a slip knot loop with the cut tail rather than the ball end (figure 1). Work into loop as follows: **[yo, k1]** until desired even number of stitches has been cast on (figure 2).

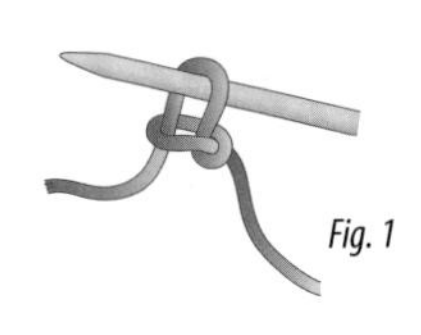

Fig. 1

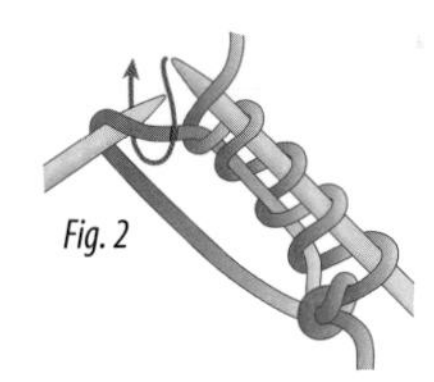

Fig. 2

Stitch Key
KOK
Knit corner stitch
Purl corner stitch
Knit
Purl
Color Key
Greystone Heather (A)
Jet (B)
Repeat 4x

Tibetan Rose
125 yds

4.5mm/US 7
or size to obtain gauge

Kathleen Power Johnson

SARASOTA, FLORIDA

*This embossed diagonal counterpane block pattern is a fusion of the simple "Bassett Pattern" in **Mary Walker Phillips' Knitting Counterpanes** with the intricate embossed effects typical of many counterpane motif designs. Leaves are among the most common embossed details in this knitting genre. I chose a contemporary lacy leaf to complement the recurring mesh pattern. Bobbles are the real heavyweights in embossed motifs. Here, 4-stitch bobbles are grouped at one corner. Picture an actual counterpane where this square would be joined with 3 others: the bobble clusters would form a dense centerpiece flanked by the delicate leaf elements converging in radiating squares. The lattice-like mesh contributes a delicate overall balance.*

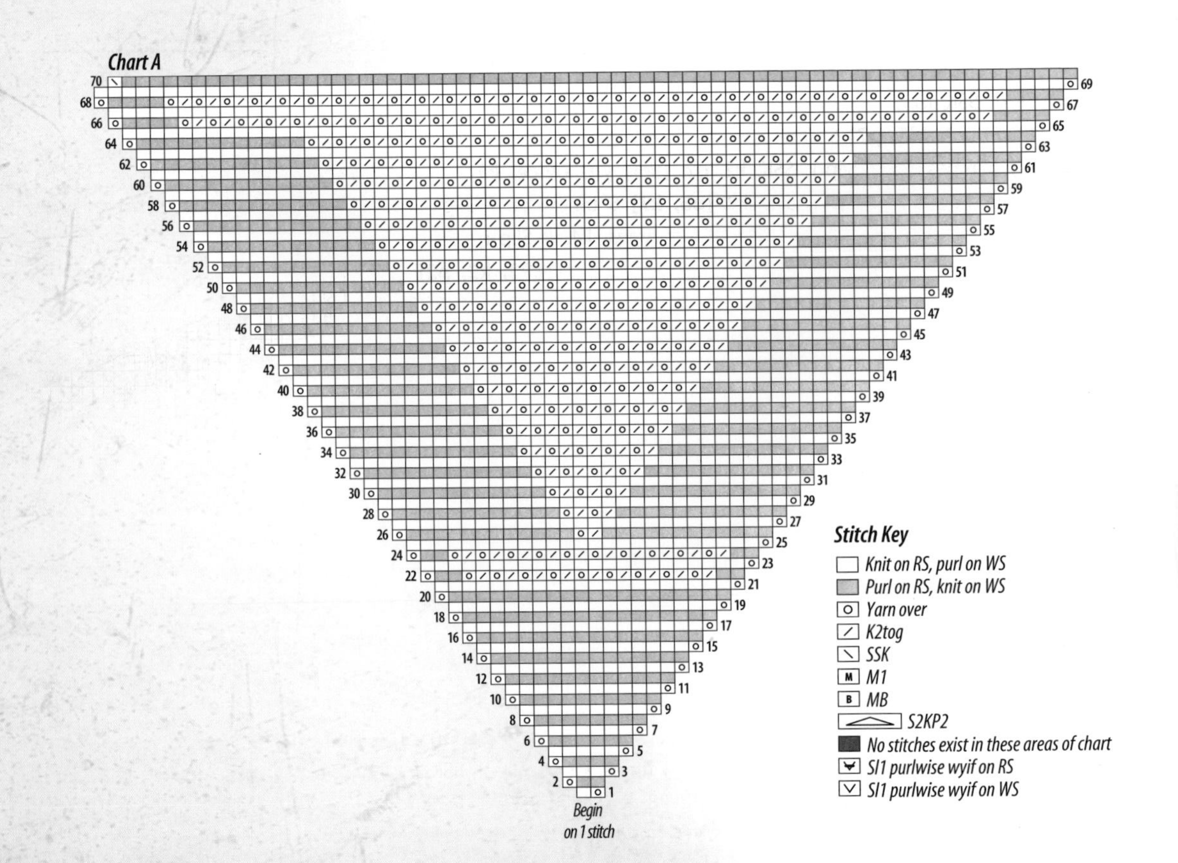

Notes 1 *See page 52 for unfamiliar abbreviations and techniques.*
2 *For ease in working, mark RS of square.*

Square

Cast on 1. Work 70 rows of Chart A — 69 stitches. Work 67 rows of Chart B. Fasten off last stitch.

Finishing

Damp block to 12" square.

IN OTHER WORDS

MAKE BOBBLE (MB) Knit into front, back, front, back of stitch, turn; slip 1, p3, turn; slip 1, k3, turn; slip 1, p3, turn; slip 2 together knitwise, k2tog, P2SSO.

CHART A *BEGIN ON 1 STITCH*

Row 1 (RS) Yo, k1. 2 Yo, k2. 3–21 Yo, knit to end — 22 stitches at end of Row 21. 22, 24 Yo, k2, ***[yo, k2tog]** to last 2 stitches, k2. 23 and all following RS rows Yo, knit to end. 26 Yo, k12, place marker (pm), yo, k2tog, pm, k12. 28 Yo, k12, **[yo, k2tog]** twice, k12. WS rows 30–64 (RS) Yo, k12 **[yo, k2tog]** to marker, k12. Remove markers. 66, 68 Yo, k4, ***[yo, k2tog]** to last 4 stitches, k4. 70 SSK, knit to end — 69 stitches.

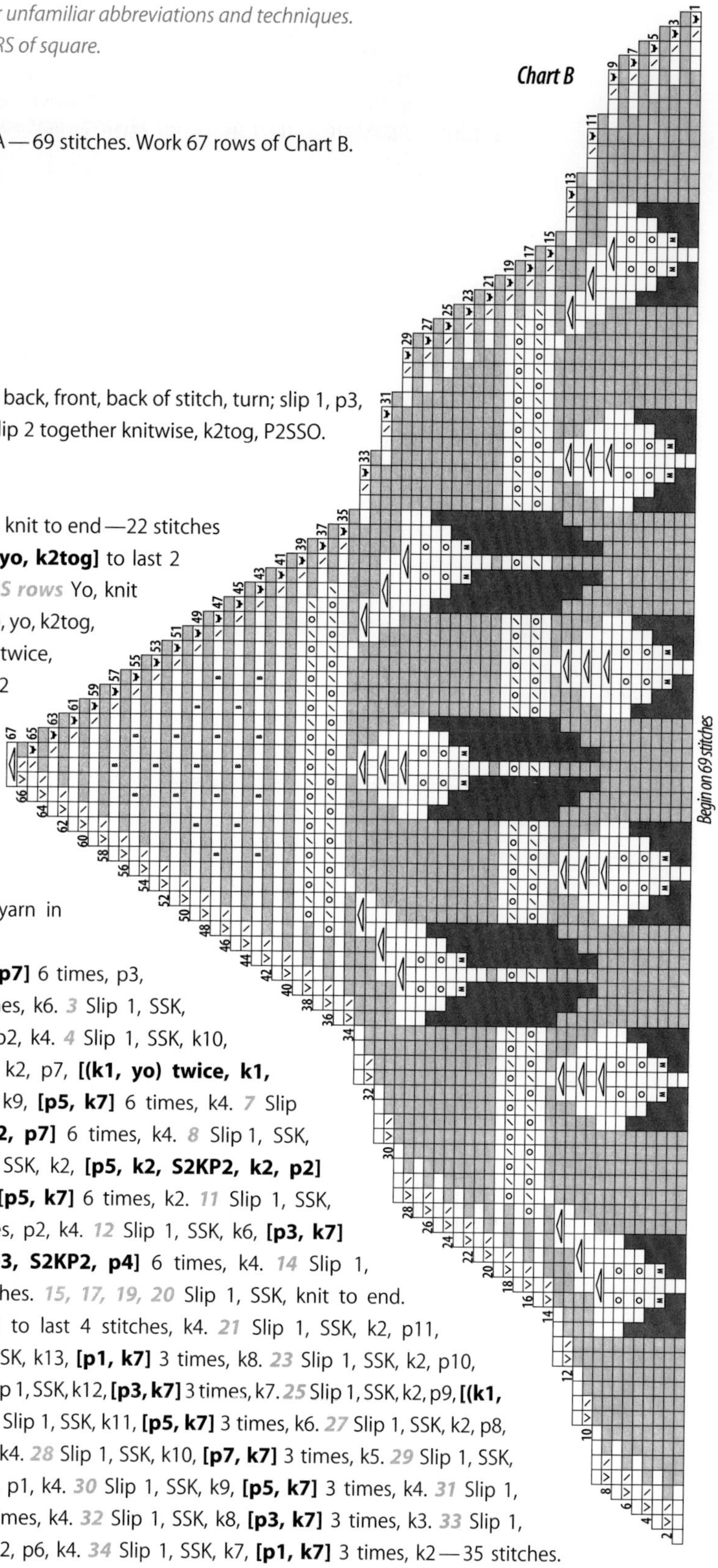

CHART B *BEGIN ON 69 STITCHES*

Note Slip all stitches purlwise with yarn in front.

Row 1 (RS) Slip 1, SSK, k2, p9, **[k1, p7]** 6 times, p3, k4. 2 Slip1, SSK, k11, **[p1, k7]** 6 times, k6. 3 Slip 1, SSK, k2, p8, **[M1, k1, M1, p7]** 6 times, p2, k4. 4 Slip 1, SSK, k10, **[p3, k7]** 6 times, k5. 5 Slip 1, SSK, k2, p7, **[(k1, yo) twice, k1, p7]** 6 times, p1, k4. 6 Slip 1, SSK, k9, **[p5, k7]** 6 times, k4. 7 Slip 1, SSK, k2, p6, **[k2, yo, k1, yo, k2, p7]** 6 times, k4. 8 Slip 1, SSK, k8, **[p7, k7]** 6 times, k3. 9 Slip 1, SSK, k2, **[p5, k2, S2KP2, k2, p2]** 6 times, p4, k4. 10 Slip 1, SSK, k7, **[p5, k7]** 6 times, k2. 11 Slip 1, SSK, k2, **[p4, k1, S2KP2, k1, p3]** 6 times, p2, k4. 12 Slip 1, SSK, k6, **[p3, k7]** 6 times, k1. 13 Slip 1, SSK, k2, **[p3, S2KP2, p4]** 6 times, k4. 14 Slip 1, SSK, k5, **[p1, k7]** 6 times — 55 stitches. 15, 17, 19, 20 Slip 1, SSK, knit to end. 16, 18 Slip 1, SSK, k3, **[yo, k2tog]** to last 4 stitches, k4. 21 Slip 1, SSK, k2, p11, **[k1, p7]** 3 times, p5, k4. 22 Slip 1, SSK, k13, **[p1, k7]** 3 times, k8. 23 Slip 1, SSK, k2, p10, **[M1, k1, M1, p7]** 3 times, p4, k4. 24 Slip 1, SSK, k12, **[p3, k7]** 3 times, k7. 25 Slip 1, SSK, k2, p9, **[(k1, yo) twice, k1, p7]** 3 times, p3, k4. 26 Slip 1, SSK, k11, **[p5, k7]** 3 times, k6. 27 Slip 1, SSK, k2, p8, **[k2, yo, k1, yo, k2, p7]** 3 times, p2, k4. 28 Slip 1, SSK, k10, **[p7, k7]** 3 times, k5. 29 Slip 1, SSK, k2, p7, **[k2, S2KP2, k2, p7]** 3 times, p1, k4. 30 Slip 1, SSK, k9, **[p5, k7]** 3 times, k4. 31 Slip 1, SSK, k2, p6, **[k1, S2KP2, k1, p7]** 3 times, k4. 32 Slip 1, SSK, k8, **[p3, k7]** 3 times, k3. 33 Slip 1, SSK, k2, p5, **[S2KP2, p7]** twice, S2KP2, p6, k4. 34 Slip 1, SSK, k7, **[p1, k7]** 3 times, k2 — 35 stitches. 35–40 Repeat Rows 15–20 — 29 stitches at end of Row 20. 41 Slip 1, SSK, knit to end. 42 and all following WS rows Repeat Row 41. 43 Slip 1, SSK, k4, **[MB, k3]** 4 times, k4. 45 Slip 1, SSK, k5, **[MB, k3]** 3 times, k5. 47 Slip 1, SSK, k2, **[MB, k3]** 4 times, k2. 49 Slip 1, SSK, k3, **[MB, k3]** 3 times, k3. 51 Slip 1, SSK, k4, **[MB, k3]** twice, k4. 53 Slip 1, SSK, k5, MB, k8. 55 Slip 1, SSK, k2, **[MB, k3]** twice, k2. 57 Slip 1, SSK, k3, MB, k6. 59, 61, 63, 65 Slip 1, SSK, knit to end. 67 S2KP2 — 1 stitch.

Chart B

Begin on 69 stitches

17

Gloria Tracy

SANTA BARBARA, CALIFORNIA

My square looks like a present and that's exactly what it is. Open up the pattern and you find—surprise!—the complex-looking finished square is really just unusual applications of a simple slip-stitch pattern and an easy seaming technique. I've chosen the Thorn Flowers pattern because it is simple—only a 4-row repeat with a 4-row offset—and shows so clearly how you can get dramatic results just by reversing colors. A common finishing technique, 3-needle bind-off, becomes a design feature simply by placing the seam on the outside and working it in a contrasting color. Enlarged, the square would make a great pillow top. A bonus gift is an easy way of working the SSKs taught to me by Hélène Rush who learned it from her French Canadian mother. Happy (fill in the blank) everyone!

A Silver
B Jet
C Tibetan Rose
50 yds each

5mm/US 8

5mm/US 8
24" (60cm) long
optional smaller needle
to pick up stitches

Crochet hook
Waste yarn
Stitch holders & markers

Note *See page 52 for unfamiliar abbreviations and techniques.*

Thorn Flowers *multiple of 4 stitches, plus 1*

Squares 1 and 3 MC=B; CC= A .
Squares 2 and 4 MC=A; CC= B .
Row 1 (RS) With MC, k2, **[KOK, k3]** to last 2 stitches, end k2. *2* With CC, p2, **[sl 3 with yarn in front (wyif), p3]** to last 2 stitches, p2. *3* With CC, k1, **[k2tog, sl 1 with yarn in back (wyib), SSK, k1]** to end. *4* With MC, p4, **[sl 1 wyif, p3]** to last 4 stitches, p4. *5* With MC, k4, **[KOK, k3]** to last 4 stitches, k4. *6* With CC, p4, **[sl 3 wyif, p3]** to last 4 stitches, p4. *7* With CC, k3, **[k2tog, sl 1 wyib, SSK, k1]** to last 3 stitches, k3. *8* With MC, p2, **[sl 1 wyif, p3]** to last 2 stitches, p2. Repeat Rows 1–8.

For each square, cast on 21 stitches with waste yarn, using crochet cast-on (see illustration). Purl 1 row with C. Work Rows 1–8 of Thorn Flower pattern 4 times, then work Rows 1–4 once more. Knit 1 row with C. Place all stitches on hold.

Square 2 | Square 3
Square 1 | Square 4
5"
4½"
Direction of knitting

Finishing

Transfer 21 stitches of Square 1 from holder to needle. Transfer cast-on stitches of Square 2 to needle as follows: Pick up purl bumps of first row of working yarn with smaller-gauge needle (removing waste yarn and being careful to pick up both end stitches) — 21 stitches. Transfer stitches to separate needle. With RS facing and C, and using 3-needle bind-off, join top edge of Square 1 with lower edge of Square 2. In same way, join top edge of Square 4 with lower edge of Square 3. With RS facing and C, pick up and k21 evenly along right edge of Square 1, k1 in bind-off ridge, then 21 along right edge of Square 2 — 43 stitches. Repeat for left edges of Squares 3 and 4. Join all squares using 3-needle bind-off.

Border

With RS facing, circular needle and C, and beginning at upper right corner of Square 3, **[knit across stitches on holder, pick up and k1 in bind-off ridge, knit across stitches on holder, place marker (pm) for corner, pick up and knit 43 along next edge, pm]** twice — 172 stitches. Join and purl 1 round. *Next round* Knit, increase 1 stitch each side of each marker — 180 stitches. Purl 1 round. Repeat last 2 rounds twice more, binding off 196 stitches purlwise on last round. With 3 strands of C held together, tie a bow and attach to center of square.

crochet cast-on

1 Leaving short tail, make slip knot on crochet hook. Hold crochet hook in right hand and knitting needle on top of yarn in left hand. With hook to right of yarn, bring yarn through loop on hook; yarn goes over top of needle forming a stitch.

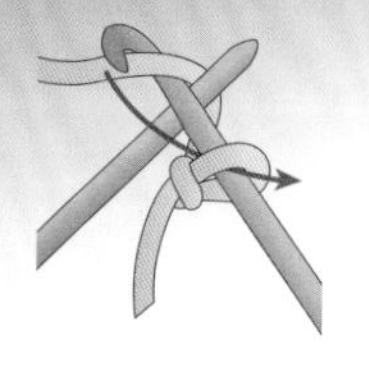

2 Bring yarn under point of needle and hook yarn through loop forming next stitch.

Repeat Step 2 to last stitch. Slip loop from hook to needle for last stitch.

simplified SSK

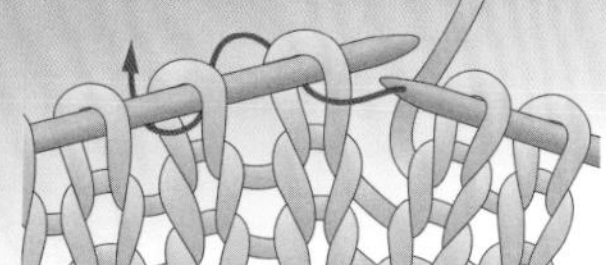

1 Insert right needle into front of first stitch, then into back of second stitch.

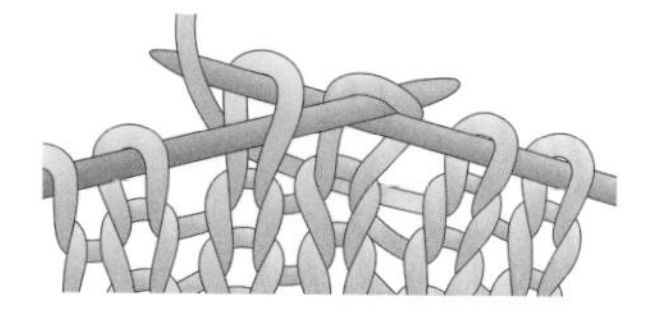

2 Knit these 2 stitches together.

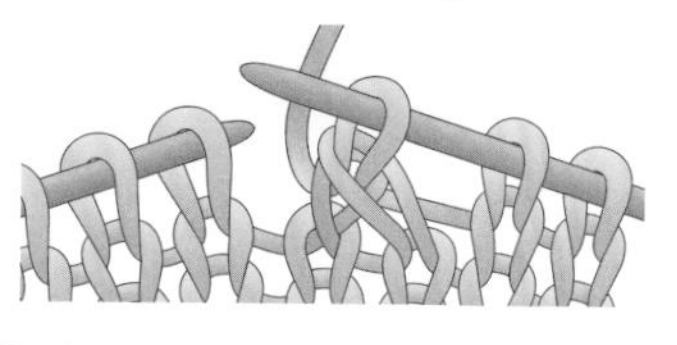

3 The result is a left-slanting decrease. The second stitch is twisted and sits neatly under the first stitch.

18

Anna Zilboorg

MEADOWS OF DAN, VIRGINIA

Garter and slip stitch couldn't be simpler technically. The complexity comes from following the charts. This is easier than at first glance if, instead of counting the stitches to be knit, you simply note where they line up with previously slipped stitches of the same color, or where the stitches you are going to slip line up with previously knit stitches. If you discover that you've made a mistake, it's easy to drop a stitch down any number of ridges and pick it back up the way you want (use a crochet hook!).

Notes **1** *See page 52 for unfamiliar abbreviations and techniques.* **2** *Separate yarn B into 3 balls: 1 large and 2 small.*

MOSAIC CHART NOTES

1 *Each chart row consists of knit stitches and slip stitches (or just knit stitches). One color is worked each pair of rows. That color is shown in the column at the right of chart.* ***Rows 1 and 2*** *Work with B: Knit B stitches, slip A stitches purlwise with yarn at WS of work.* ***Rows 3 and 4*** *Work with A: Knit A stitches, slip B stitches.*

2 *Each chart row is worked twice, once on RS; then on WS, knitting or slipping the same stitches as on the RS row.*

3 *Use separate ball of yarn for each large block of color, as instructed.*

A Greystone Heather
B Cerise
75 yds each

10cm/4"
40 [gauge grid] **18**
over Chart pattern

5mm/US 8
or size to obtain gauge

&
tapestry needle
4 split stitch markers

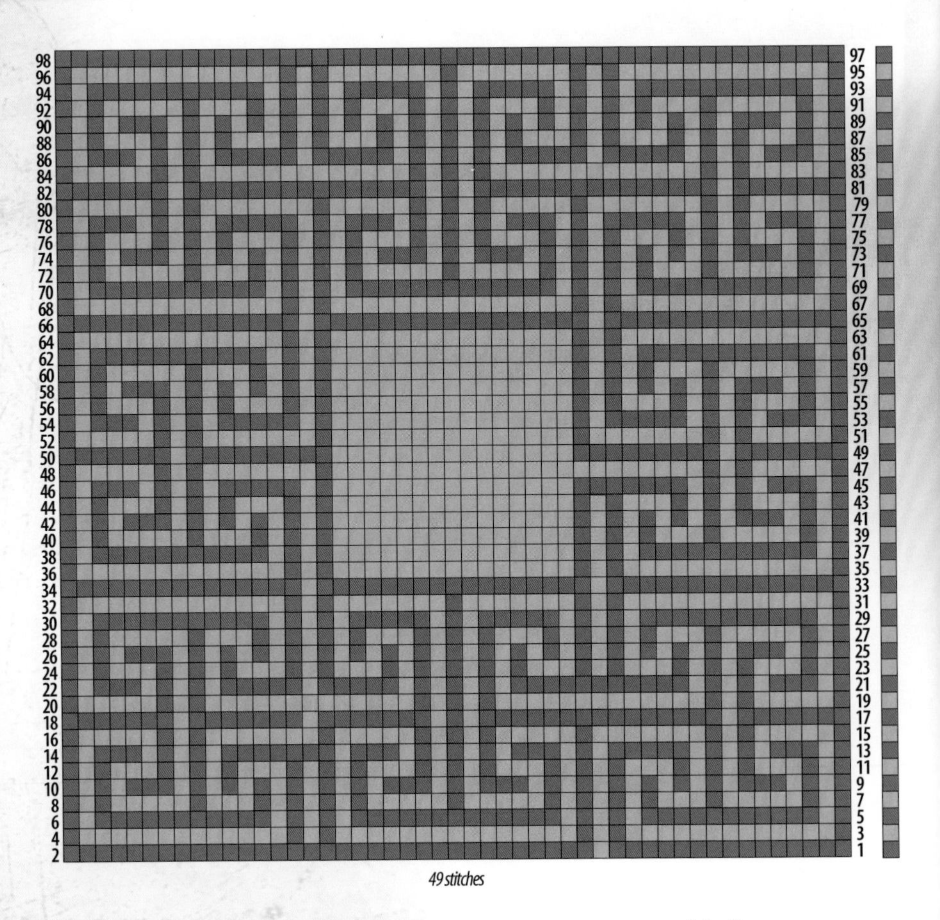

Color Key
Greystone Heather (A)
Tibetan Rose (B)

Square

With A, cast on 55. Knit 5 rows. ***Begin Chart: Row 1*** (RS) K3A, join B and work Row 1 over center 49 stitches, join 2nd ball of A and knit remaining 3 stitches. ***2*** K3A, with B work Row 2 to last 3 stitches, k3A. ***3, 4*** Work with same ball of A across entire row as follows: k3, work Chart over 49 stitches, k3. Continue as established, working A rows with 1 ball and B rows with 3 balls, through Row 36. ***Row 37*** (RS) K3A, with B, work first 17 stitches of chart, join separate ball of A and k15, join separate ball of B and work to last 3 stitches, k3A. Continue in pattern, working A rows with 1 ball and B rows with 5 balls, through Row 62. Cut 2 center balls and work as before through Row 98. With A, knit 5 rows. Bind off.

19

Lois Young

HOUGHTON, MICHIGAN

My square uses texture to show a blossoming vine. I like curves and flowers, and this vine is a good way to incorporate both. The vines look like traveling stitch, but in fact are a paired increase and decrease. I find that the stems lie flatter with this method of traveling, and the traveling stitch doesn't get elongated. The chart is written for right-handed knitters, but it can be worked left-handed if the SSK is worked as a k2tog and vice versa.

Note *See page 52 for unfamiliar abbreviations and techniques.*

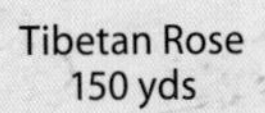

Tibetan Rose
150 yds

10cm/4"

27 / 19
over Chart pattern

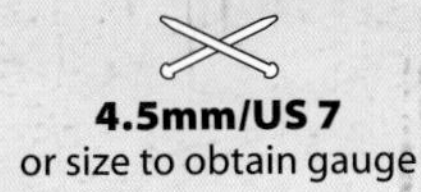

4.5mm/US 7
or size to obtain gauge

Square

Cast on 57. Knit 5 rows, end with a RS row. Keeping first and last 3 stitches in garter stitch (knit every row), work center 51 stitches in chart pattern as follows: ***Row 1*** (WS) Reading chart from left to right, work 12-stitch repeat 4 times, then work last 3 stitches. Continue in pattern as established through Row 71. Knit 5 rows. Bind off.

IN OTHER WORDS

Chart *over 51 stitches*

Row 1 (WS) **[K5, p1, k6]** 4 times, k3. *2* P3, **[p5, k2tog, M1L, p5]** 4 times. *3* **[K6, p1, k5]** 4 times, k3. *4* P3, **[p4, k2tog, M1L, p6]** 4 times. *5* **[K7, p1, k4]** 4 times, k3. *6* P3, **[p3, k2tog, M1L, p7]** 4 times. *7* **[K8, p1, k3]** 4 times, k3. *8* P3, **[p2, k2, p8]** 4 times. *9* **[K8, p3, k1]** 4 times, k3. *10* P3, **[k3, M1R, SSK, p7]** 4 times. *11* **[K7, p1, k1, p3]** 4 times, k3. *12* P3, **[k3, p1, M1R, SSK, p6]** 4 times. *13* **[K6, p1, k2, p3]** 4 times, k3. *14* P3, **[k2, p3, M1R, SSK, p5]** 4 times. *15* **[K5, p1]** 8 times, k3. *16* P3, **[p6, k1, p5]** 4 times. *17* **[K5, p1, k6]** 4 times, k3. *18* P3, **[p5, k2tog, M1L, p5]** 4 times. *19* **[K6, p1, k5]** 4 times, k3. *20* P3, **[p4, k2tog, M1L, k1, p5]** 4 times. *21* **[K5, p1, k1, p1, k4]** 4 times, k3. *22* P3, **[p3, k2tog, M1L, k3, p4]** 4 times. *23* **[K4, p3, k1, p1, k3]** 4 times, k3. *24* P3, **[p2, k2tog, M1L, k5, p3]** 4 times. *25 and 27* **[K3, p5, k1, p1, k2]** 4 times, k3. *26* P3, **[p2, k1, p1, k5, p3]** 4 times. *28* P3, **[p2, (k1, p1) 4 times, p2]** 4 times. *29* **[K3, (p1, k1) 4 times, k1]** 4 times, k3. *30* P3, **[p2, k1, p3, k1, p5]** 4 times. *31* **[K9, p1, k2]** 4 times, k3. *32* P3, **[p2, M1R, SSK, p8]** 4 times. *33* **[K8, p1, k3]** 4 times, k3. *34* P3, **[p3, M1R, SSK, p7]** 4 times. *35* **[K7, p1, k4]** 4 times, k3. *36* P3, **[p4, M1R, SSK, p6]** 4 times. *37* **[K6, p1, k5]** 4 times, k3. *38* P3, **[p5, k2, p5]** 4 times. *39* **[K4, p3, k5]** 4 times, k3. *40* P3, **[p4, k2tog, M1L, k3, p3]** 4 times. *41* **[K3, p3, k1, p1, k4]** 4 times, k3. *42* P3, **[p3, k2tog, M1L, p1, k3, p3]** 4 times. *43* **[K3, p3, k2, p1, k3]** 4 times, k3. *44* P3, **[p2, k2tog, M1L, p3, k2, p3]** 4 times. *45* **[K3, p1, k5, p1, k2]** 4 times, k3. *46* P3, **[p2, k1, p9]** 4 times. *47* **[K9, p1, k2]** 4 times, k3. *48* P3, **[p2, M1R, SSK, p8]** 4 times. *49* **[K8, p1, k3]** 4 times, k3. *50* P3, **[p2, k1, M1R, SSK, p7]** 4 times. *51* **[K7, p1, k1, p1, k2]** 4 times, k3. *52* P3, **[p1, k3, M1R, SSK, p6]** 4 times. *53* **[K6, p1, k1, p3, k1]** 4 times, k3. *54* P3, **[k5, M1R, SSK, p5]** 4 times. *55 and 57* **[K5, p1, k1, p5]** 4 times, k3. *56* P3, **[k5, p1, k1, p5]** 4 times. *58* P3, **[(k1, p1) 4 times, p4]** 4 times. *59* **[K5, (p1, k1) 3 times, p1]** 4 times, k3. *60* P3, **[p2, k1, p2, k2tog, M1L, p5]** 4 times. *61* **[K6, p1, k5]** 4 times, k3. *62* P3, **[p4, k2tog, M1L, p6]** 4 times. *63* **[K7, p1, k4]** 4 times, k3. *64* P3, **[p2, k1, k2tog, M1L, p7]** 4 times. *65* **[K8, p3, k1]** 4 times, k3. *66* P3, **[k4, p8]** 4 times. *67* **[K9, p3]** 4 times, k3. *68* P3, **[k2, p10]** 4 times. *69* **[K11, p1]** 4 times, k3. *70* Purl. *71* Knit.

Stitch Key
Knit on RS, purl on WS
Knit on WS, purl on RS
K2tog
SSK
M1L
M1R
12-stitch repeat

20

Rita Garrity Knudson

GOLDEN VALLEY, MINNESOTA

A German pharmacist taught me to knit on December 6, 1984, and I have been knitting ever since. I love everything about knitting and find it to be the most enjoyable craft I have ever tried.

I wanted my square to be knit circularly. I started with the outer perimeter and worked my way toward the center. A square is created by decreasing at 4 evenly-spaced points. I wanted to use most of the colors used in the Great North American Afghan. I love gingham and decided to offset the square with it. The colors reminded me of roses so I graphed a rambling rose pattern to frame a bullion-stitch rose.

MC Silver
125 yds

A Greystone Heather
B Jet
C Flamingo Pink
F Celtic Green
25 yds each

D Tibetan Rose
E Cerise
10 yds each

4.5mm/US 7
24" (60cm) long
or size to obtain gauge

5 **4.5mm/US 7**

Tapestry needle

Notes

1 *See page 52 for unfamiliar abbreviations and techniques.* **2** *Change to dpn when necessary.*

Square

With circular needle and MC, cast on 240 stitches. Join and work in rounds as follows: *Round 1* **[Work Round 1 of chart over 60 stitches]** 4 times. Continue in pattern through Chart Round 45—8 stitches. Cut yarn, leaving a 6" tail. With tapestry needle, draw tail through remaining stitches twice, pull snug. and fasten off.

Finishing

Duplicate stitch rose pattern on Rounds 20–29, following chart. Using photo as guide, use bullion stitch and work rose in center of square, starting with D, then working outward with E, then C.

Bullion stitch

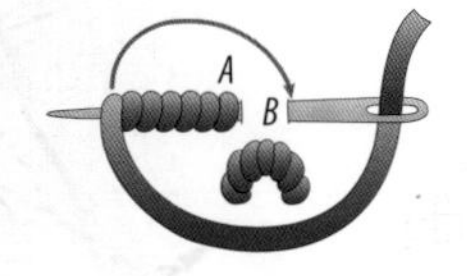

Leaf *make 4 with F*

Cast on 3 stitches. Work Chart B. Fasten off last stitch. Using photo as guide, sew leaves over decrease stitches around bullion rose.

IN OTHER WORDS

S2KP2 Slip 2 stitches together knitwise, k1, P2SSO.

CHART A *Begin on 240 stitches*

Round 1 With MC, **[p59, k1]** 4 times. *2* Knit. *3* P1, **[p57, S2KP2]** 4 times. *4* K1, **[k55, S2KP2]** 4 times. *5* **[P55, k1]** 4 times. *6* K1, **[k53, S2KP2]** 4 times. *7* K1MC, **[(k2A, k2MC) 12 times, k2A, k1MC, S2KP2]** 4 times. *8* **[K2A, k2MC]** around. *9* K1B, **[k1B, (k2A, k2B) 12 times, S2KP2]** 4 times. *10* K1B, **[(k2A, k2B) 11 times, k2A, k1B, S2KP2]** 4 times. *11* **[K2MC, k2A]** around. *12* K1MC, **[k1MC, (k2A, k2MC) 11 times, S2KP2]** 4 times.

Note Work remaining rounds with MC only. *13* K1, **[k43, S2KP2]** 4 times. *14* **[P43, k1]** 4 times. *15* K1, **[k41, S2KP2]** 4 times. *16* P1, **[p39, S2KP2]** 4 times. *17* Knit. *18* P1, **[p37, S2KP2]** 4 times. *19* K1, **[k35, S2KP2]** 4 times. *20* Knit. *21* K1, **[k33, S2KP2]** 4 times. *22* K1, **[k31, S2KP2]** 4 times. *23* Knit. *24* K1, **[k29, S2KP2]** 4 times. *25* K1, **[k27, S2KP2]** 4 times. *26* Knit. *27* K1, **[k25, S2KP2]** 4 times. *28* K1, **[k23, S2KP2]** 4 times. *29* Knit. *30* P1, **[p21, S2KP2]** 4 times. *31* K1, **[k19, S2KP2]** 4 times. *32* **[P19, k1]** 4 times. *33* K1, **[k17, S2KP2]** 4 times. *34* P1, **[p15, S2KP2]** 4 times. *35* Knit. *36* K1, **[k13, S2KP2]** 4 times. *37* K1, **[k11, S2KP2]** 4 times. *38* Knit. *39* K1, **[k9, S2KP2]** 4 times. *40* K1, **[k7, S2KP2]** 4 times. *41* Knit. *42* K1, **[k5, S2KP2]** 4 times. *43* K1, **[k3, S2KP2]** 4 times. *44* Knit. *45* K1, **[k1, S2KP2]** 4 times.

Chart B *begin on 3 stitches*

Note Slip stitches purlwise with yarn at WS of work.

Row 1 (WS) P3. *2* **[K1, M1]** twice, k1—5 stitches. *3* P2, slip 1, p2. 4 K1, M1, k3, M1, k1—7 stitches. *5, 7* P3, slip 1, p3. *6* K7. *8* K1, SSK, k1, k2tog, k1—5 stitches. *9* Repeat row 3. *10* K1, S2KP2, k1—3 stitches. *11* P3. *12* S2KP2.

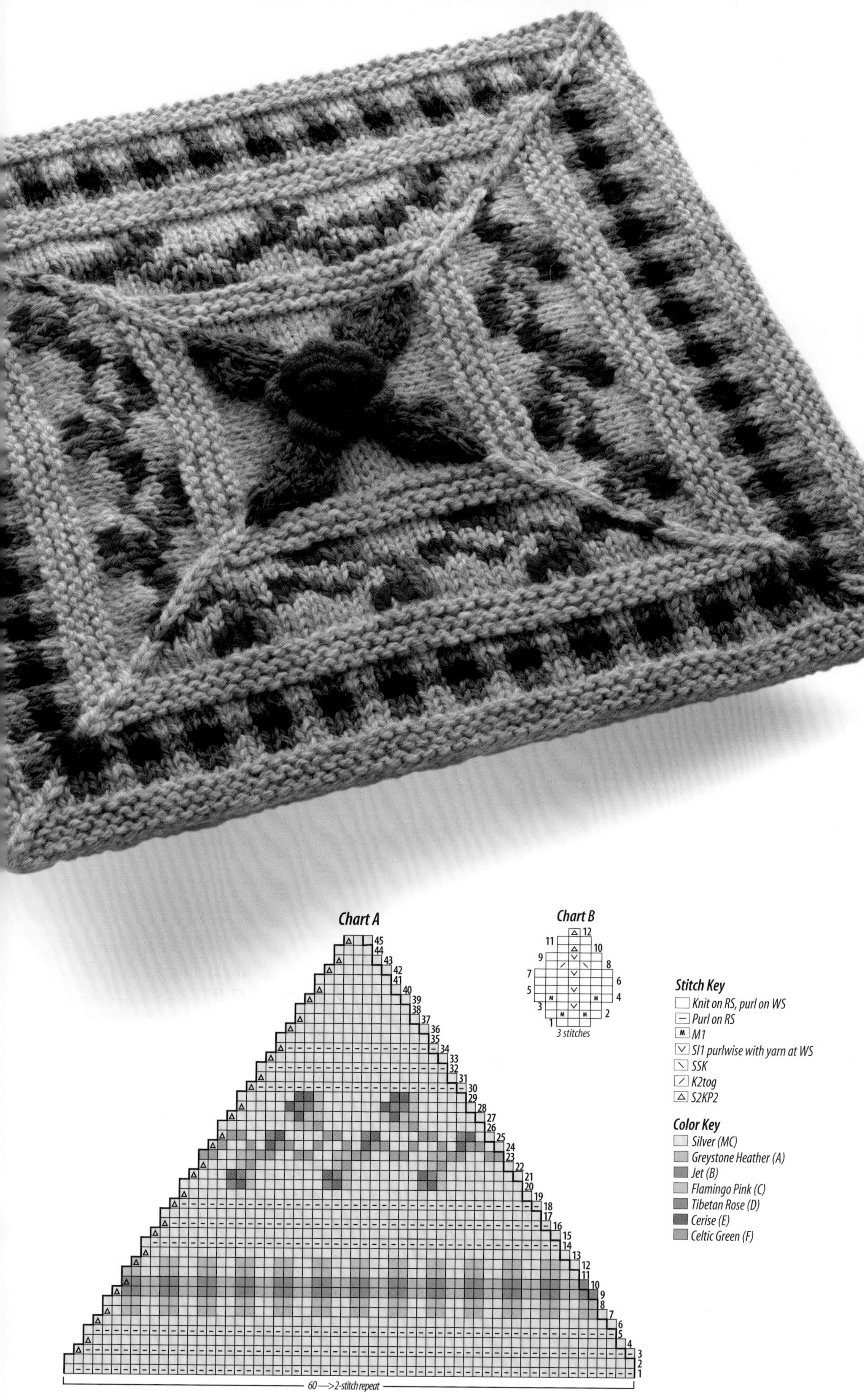

Chart Note *Work Chart A Rounds 20–29 with MC only; work rambling rose pattern in duplicate stitch after square is completed.*

21

Lyn Youll

TORONTO, ONTARIO

I was born in England and was taught to knit by my grandmother, an avid knitter, when I was very young. I've made my home in North America, but sometimes I dream of living in a little cottage somewhere in England. In this afghan square I was able to combine my love of knitting and embroidery with my little dream cottage. I hope that you enjoy knitting it as much as I did!

MC Silver
100 yds

A Greystone Heather
B Jet
C Cerise
25 yds each

D Flamingo Pink
E Tibetan Rose
F Celtic Green
10 yds each

4.5mm/US 7
or size to obtain gauge

Notes 1 *See page 52 for unfamiliar abbreviations and techniques.* **2** *When working Chart Rows 3–16 and Row 47, carry colors across WS of work; on Rows 21–40 and 48–72, use separate balls of yarn for each block of color.*

1/1 RT K2tog, leave on left needle, knit first stitch again, slip both stitches off needle.

Square

With MC, cast on 58. Work 2 ridges, end with a WS row. Keeping first and last 3 stitches in garter stitch, work center 52 stitches of Chart through Row 74. With MC, work 2 ridges. Bind off all stitches.

Finishing

With B, work duplicate stitch window boxes over 9 stitches and 2 rows marked at bottom of both windows. Using photo as guide and D and E, work French knot flowers along bottom of fence, in window boxes, and around door. With F, work straight stitch leaves on flowers.

DUPLICATE STITCH

With a blunt tapestry needle threaded with a length of yarn of a contrasting color, cover a knitted stitch with an embroidered stitch of the same shape.

Straight stitch

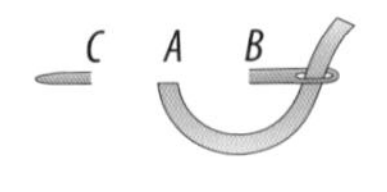

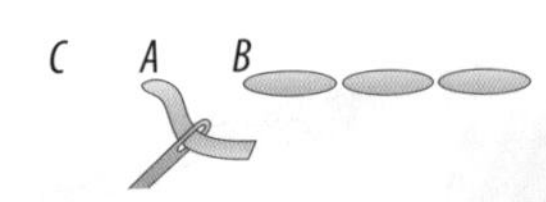

French knot

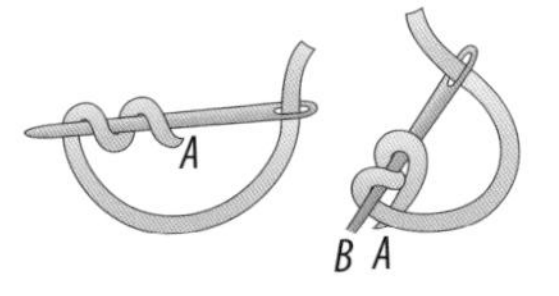

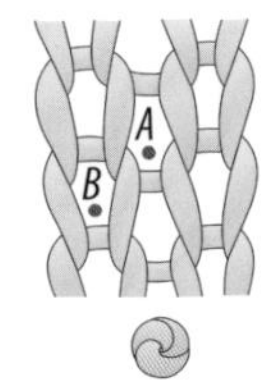

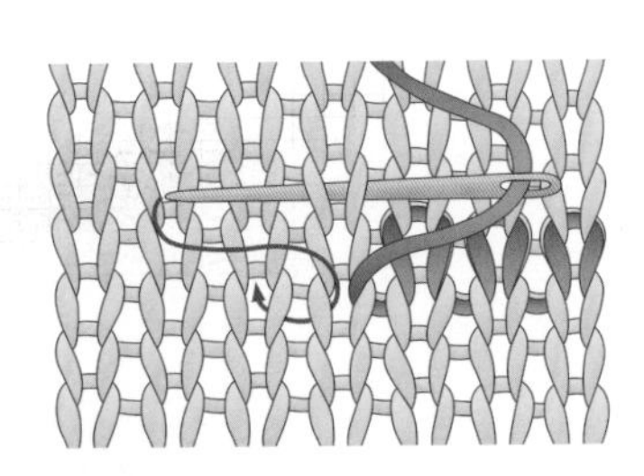

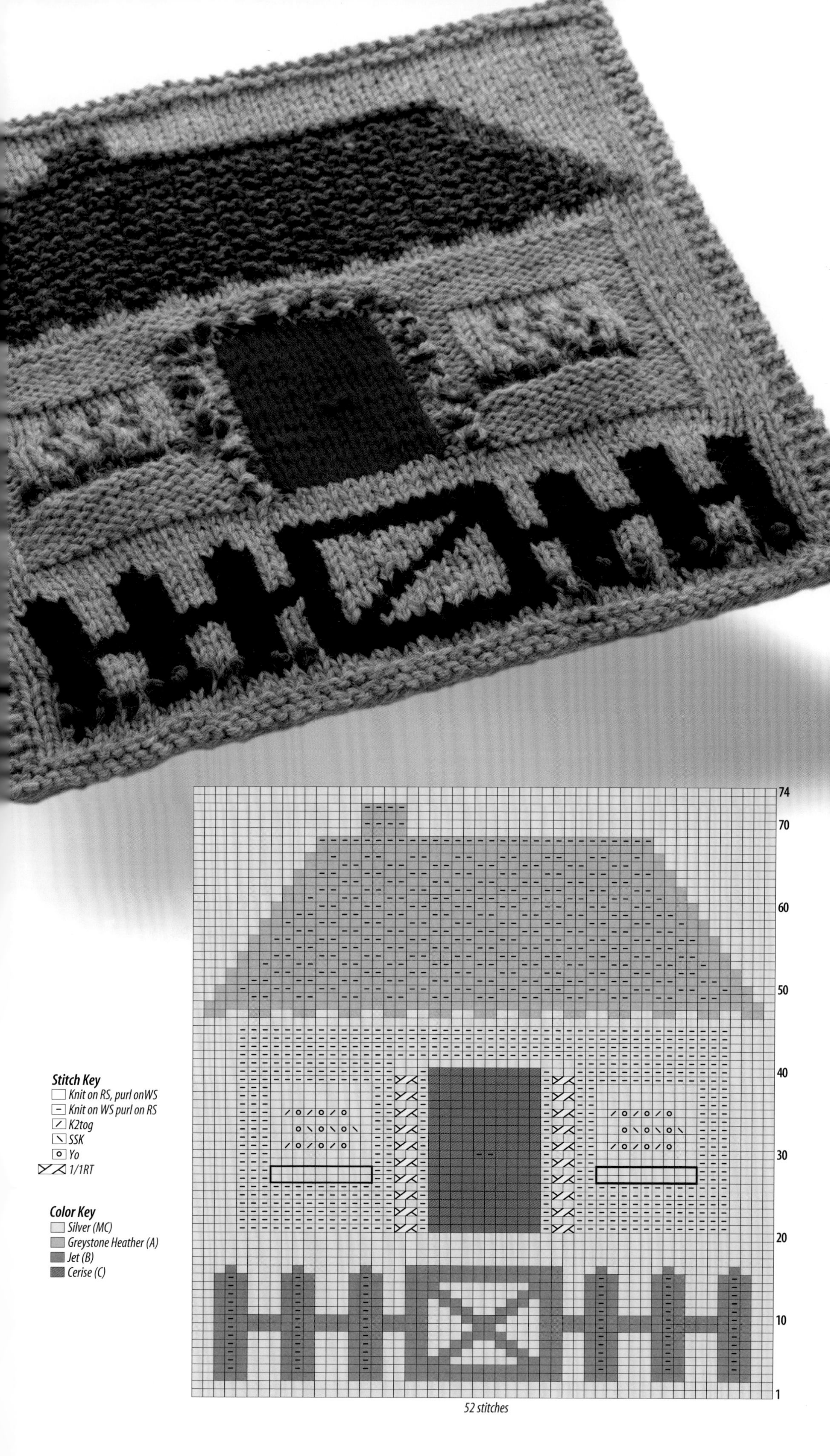
Stitch Key
Knit on RS, purl onWS
Knit on WS purl on RS
K2tog
SSK
Yo
1/1RT
Color Key
Silver (MC)
Greystone Heather (A)
Jet (B)
Cerise (C)
74
70
60
50
40
30
20
10
1
52 stitches

22

Gayle Bunn

TORONTO, ONTARIO

This square combines my favorite knitting techniques with inspiration from vintage knitwear. Cables and Fair Isle are mediums in which I love to design and knit. The rose is in honor of the many gardens from my past (my father is also a landscape designer) and my present. I worked the rose in duplicate stitch, a technique very similar to needlepoint, another of my favorite crafts.

MC Silver
100 yds

A Greystone Heather
B Tibetan Rose
25 yds each

C Flamingo Pink
D Cerise
E Celtic Green
10 yds each

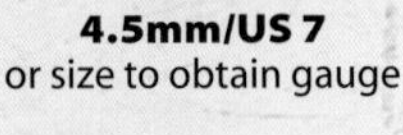

4.5mm/US 7
or size to obtain gauge

• Cable needle (cn)

Notes **1** *See page 52 for unfamiliar abbreviations and techniques. See page 27 for pick up and knit.* **2** *Square is made in sections: cable strips, center square, and side borders.*

Square

CABLE STRIP *make 4*

With MC, cast on 2. ***Work Chart A*** Work Rows 1–19, **[work Rows 12–19]** 7 times, work Rows 20–35. Fasten off.

CENTER SQUARE

With A, cast on 37. Knit 1 row. Purl 1 row. ***Begin Chart B: Row 1*** (RS) **[Work Chart stitches 1–8]** 4 times, work stitches 1–5. Work through Row 3. With A, purl 2 rows, decrease 2 stitches on 2nd row — 35 stitches. With MC, work 41 rows in stockinette stitch. With A, knit 3 rows, increase 2 stitches on first row — 37 stitches. ***Begin Chart B: Row 1*** (WS) Reading chart from left to right, work Chart stitches 5–1, **[work stitches 8–1]** 4 times. Work through Row 3. With A, work 2 rows in stockinette stitch. Bind off.

SIDE BORDERS

With RS facing and A, pick up and knit 45 evenly along side of center square. Knit 2 rows. ***Begin Chart B: Row 1*** (WS) **[Work chart stitches 9–2]** 5 times, work stitches 9–5. Work through Row 3. With A, work 2 rows in stockinette stitch. Bind off. Repeat for other side.

Finishing

Work Chart C in duplicate stitch over MC portion of center square. Sew cable strips to sides of square. Sew mitred corners.

EYELET BORDER

With RS facing and MC, pick up and knit 55 evenly along one side of square. ***Row 1*** (WS) Knit. ***2*** K1, **[yo, k2tog]** to end. ***3 and 4*** Knit. Bind off knitwise on WS. Repeat for opposite side. With RS facing, pick up and knit 59 evenly across top of square, including side borders. Work 4-row eyelet border. Repeat for lower edge.

IN OTHER WORDS

3/3 RC Slip 3 to cable needle (cn), hold to back, k3; k3 from cn.

3/3 LC Slip 3 to cn, hold to front, k3; k3 from cn.

Chart A *2 stitches, increased to 11 stitches, decreased to 1 stitch*

Row 1 (WS) K2. ***2*** K1, M1 knit (M1K), k1. ***3*** K1, M1 purl (M1P), p1, k1. ***4*** K3, M1K, k1. ***5*** K1, M1P, p3, k1. ***6*** K5, M1K, k1. ***7*** K1, M1P, p5, k1. ***8*** K7, M1K, k1. ***9*** K1, M1P, p7, k1. ***10*** K1, 3/3 RC, k2, M1K, k1. ***11, 13, 15, 17, 19*** K1, p9, k1. ***12, 16*** Knit. ***14*** K4, 3/3 LC, k1. ***18*** K1, 3/3 RC, k4. ***20, 24*** Knit. ***21, 23, 25*** K1, p9, k1. ***22*** K4, 3/3 LC, k1. ***26*** K1, 3/3 RC, k1, k2tog, k1. ***27*** K1, p2tog, p6, k1. ***28*** K6, k2tog, k1. ***29*** K1, p2tog, p4, k1. ***30*** K4, k2tog, k1. ***31*** K1, p2tog, p2, k1. ***32*** K2, k2tog, k1. ***33*** K1, p2tog, k1. ***34*** K1, k2tog. ***35*** P2tog.

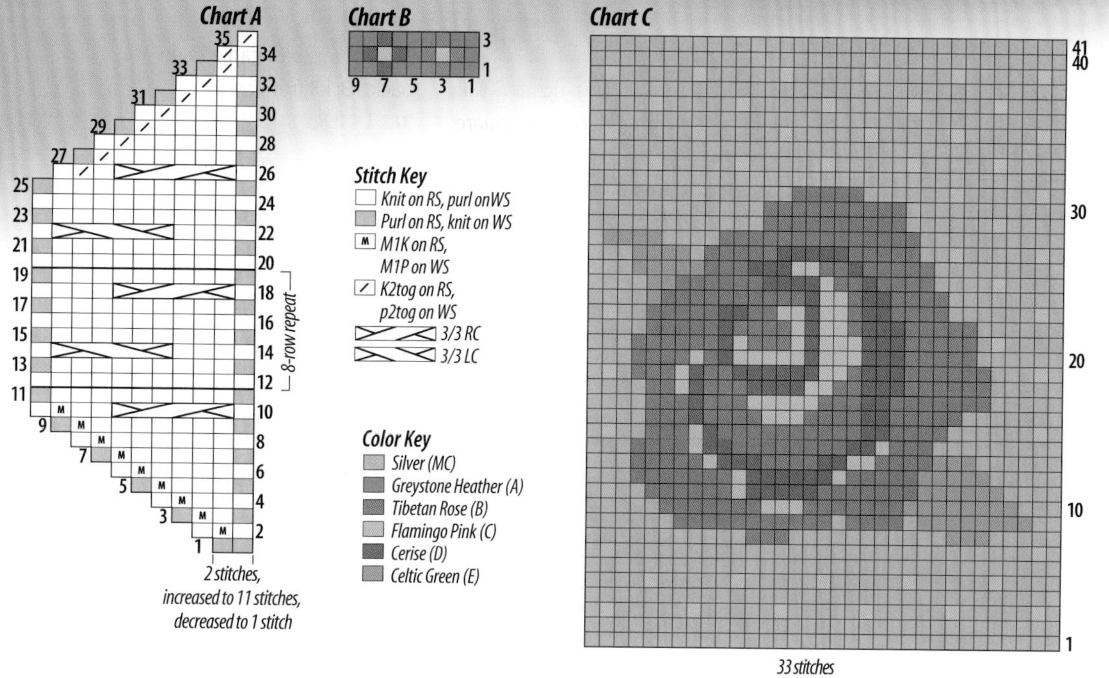

Note: *Work Chart C in duplicate stitch after square is complete.*

23

Leigh Witchel

NEW YORK, NEW YORK

My inspiration for this square came about through the afghan title and the yarn colors. A Great American Afghan, like a Great American Novel, makes me think of a broad scope, and I wanted to use a traditional American needlecraft in an updated fashion. I began to think of wedding cakes and gifts and decided to knit a cake! In fact, it would make an excellent wedding present if made into a pillow.

This square is active visually, but not difficult. All the colorwork is slip stitch using 1 color per row. It is worked from the center out with the central cast-on made easier by knitting a rose and casting on the square from it. I hope these design features will make it as enjoyable to knit as it was to design.

A Tibetan Rose
B Silver
C Flamingo Pink
50 yds each

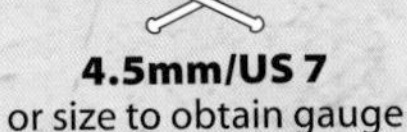

4.5mm/US 7
or size to obtain gauge

4mm/US 6
16" (40cm) and
24" (60cm) long

5 **4mm/US 6**
or size to obtain gauge

Stitch markers

Notes 1 *See page 52 for unfamiliar abbreviations and techniques.* **2** *Slip all stitches purlwise.* **3** *Begin Main Square on dpn. Change to circular needle, when there are enough stitches, placing a marker after last stitch of each dpn.*

Center Rose

PETAL 1

With A, cast on 1 and knit into front and back of stitch (Inc1) — 2 stitches. Work 15 rows of Chart A. ***Row 16*** Pick up and knit 1 from straight edge at beginning of petal (forming a small circle) — 2 stitches. ***Row 17*** K2tog. Do not fasten off; leave stitch on hold.

PETAL 2

Cast on 1 and Inc 1 — 2 stitches. Work Rows 1–7 of Chart A. Work Chart Row 8 as follows: K4, with right needle, pick up and knit 1 from straight edge of previous petal at point as shown on Rose Diagram. Place stitch on left needle and k2tog. Work Chart Rows 9–15. ***Row 16*** Pick up and knit 1 from straight edge at beginning of petal. ***Row 17*** K2tog. Do not fasten off; leave stitch on hold.

PETAL 3

Repeat Petal 2 through Row 15. ***Row 16*** Pick up and knit 1 from straight edge approximately halfway around previous petal (at beginning of Petal 4). ***Row 17*** K2tog. Do not fasten off.

PETAL 4

Repeat Petal 2 through Row 15. ***Row 16*** Pick up and knit 1 from straight edge (where Petal 4 ends on diagram). Fasten off, leaving a 12" yarn tail. Draw yarn through loop. Use yarn tail to neaten base of rose with a few overcast stitches.

Main Square

With RS facing, dpn and B, pick up and knit 20 around base of rose. Divide stitches evenly among 4 dpn. Join and work in rounds as follows: ***Round 1*** Work Round 1 of Chart B over 5 stitches for each dpn. Continue in pattern through Round 51. Bind off purlwise with A.

IN OTHER WORDS

K1 FLOAT Insert right needle under float 2 rounds below and then knitwise into next stitch on left needle; knit these 2 together.

MAKE BOBBLE (MB) (**[K1, p1 3 times, k1]** in a stitch; pass first 6 stitches, one at a time, over last stitch.

Chart A *begin on 2 stitches*

Row 1 (RS) K2. ***2*** K2. ***3*** K1, M1, k1. ***4*** K3. ***5*** K2, M1, k1. ***6*** K4. ***7*** K3, M1, k1. ***8*** K5. ***9*** K2, k2tog, k1. ***10*** K4. ***11*** K1, k2tog, k1. ***12*** K3. ***13*** K1, k2tog. ***14*** K2. ***15*** K2tog.

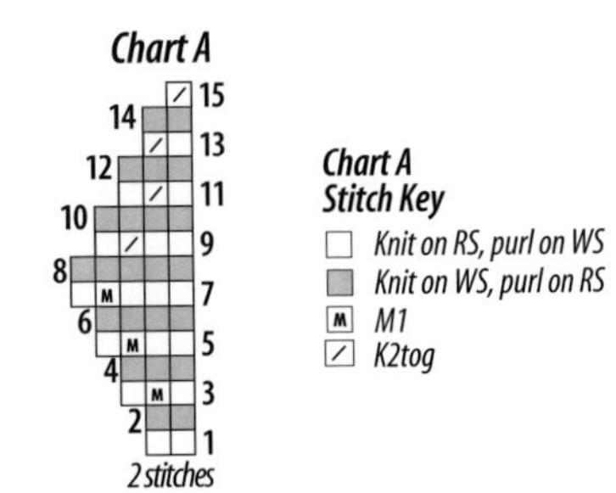

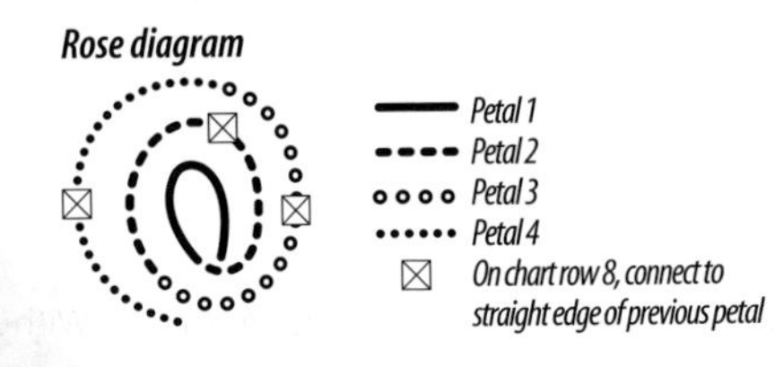

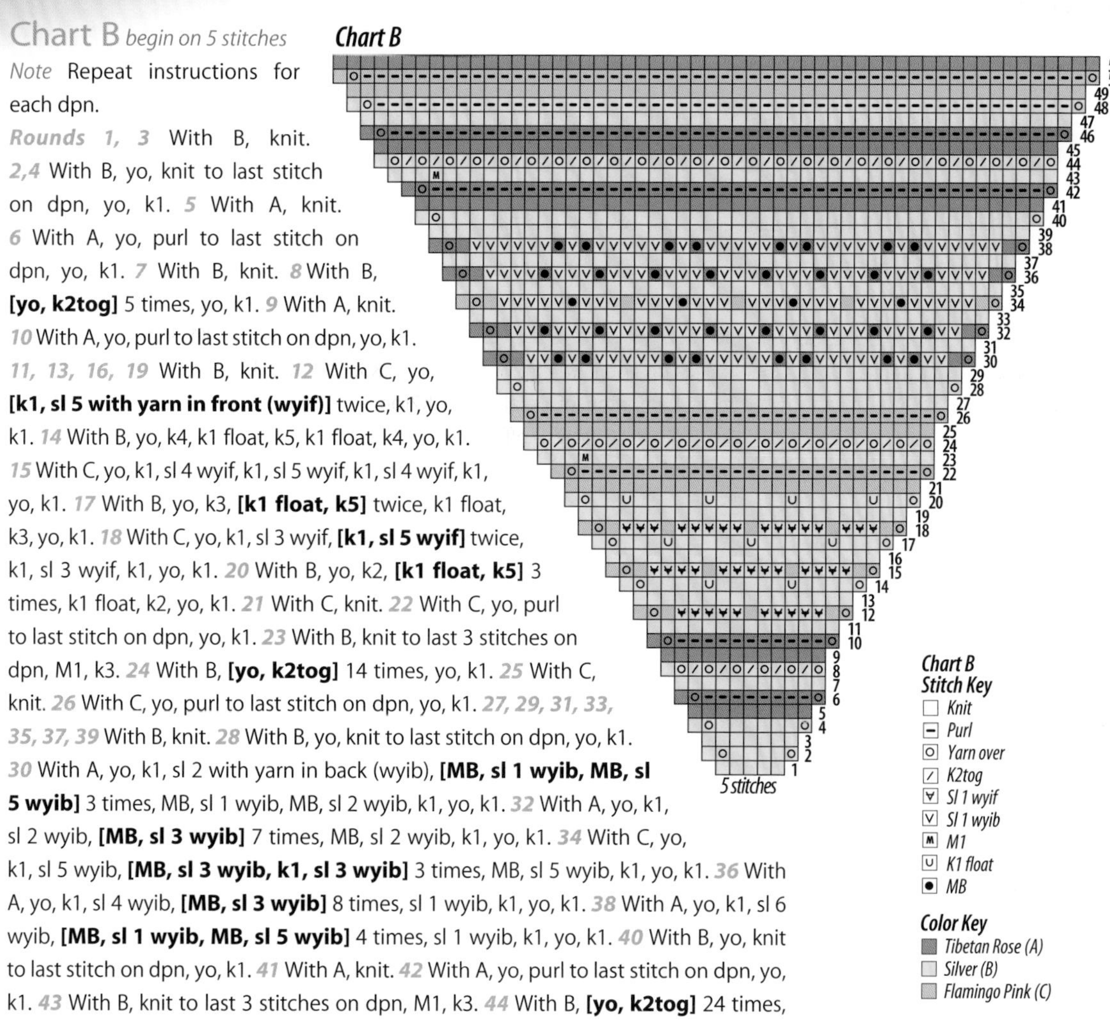

Chart B *begin on 5 stitches*

Note Repeat instructions for each dpn.

Rounds 1, 3 With B, knit. **2,4** With B, yo, knit to last stitch on dpn, yo, k1. **5** With A, knit. **6** With A, yo, purl to last stitch on dpn, yo, k1. **7** With B, knit. **8** With B, **[yo, k2tog]** 5 times, yo, k1. **9** With A, knit. **10** With A, yo, purl to last stitch on dpn, yo, k1. **11, 13, 16, 19** With B, knit. **12** With C, yo, **[k1, sl 5 with yarn in front (wyif)]** twice, k1, yo, k1. **14** With B, yo, k4, k1 float, k5, k1 float, k4, yo, k1. **15** With C, yo, k1, sl 4 wyif, k1, sl 5 wyif, k1, sl 4 wyif, k1, yo, k1. **17** With B, yo, k3, **[k1 float, k5]** twice, k1 float, k3, yo, k1. **18** With C, yo, k1, sl 3 wyif, **[k1, sl 5 wyif]** twice, k1, sl 3 wyif, k1, yo, k1. **20** With B, yo, k2, **[k1 float, k5]** 3 times, k1 float, k2, yo, k1. **21** With C, knit. **22** With C, yo, purl to last stitch on dpn, yo, k1. **23** With B, knit to last 3 stitches on dpn, M1, k3. **24** With B, **[yo, k2tog]** 14 times, yo, k1. **25** With C, knit. **26** With C, yo, purl to last stitch on dpn, yo, k1. **27, 29, 31, 33, 35, 37, 39** With B, knit. **28** With B, yo, knit to last stitch on dpn, yo, k1. **30** With A, yo, k1, sl 2 with yarn in back (wyib), **[MB, sl 1 wyib, MB, sl 5 wyib]** 3 times, MB, sl 1 wyib, MB, sl 2 wyib, k1, yo, k1. **32** With A, yo, k1, sl 2 wyib, **[MB, sl 3 wyib]** 7 times, MB, sl 2 wyib, k1, yo, k1. **34** With C, yo, k1, sl 5 wyib, **[MB, sl 3 wyib, k1, sl 3 wyib]** 3 times, MB, sl 5 wyib, k1, yo, k1. **36** With A, yo, k1, sl 4 wyib, **[MB, sl 3 wyib]** 8 times, sl 1 wyib, k1, yo, k1. **38** With A, yo, k1, sl 6 wyib, **[MB, sl 1 wyib, MB, sl 5 wyib]** 4 times, sl 1 wyib, k1, yo, k1. **40** With B, yo, knit to last stitch on dpn, yo, k1. **41** With A, knit. **42** With A, yo, purl to last stitch on dpn, yo, k1. **43** With B, knit to last 3 stitches on dpn, M1, k3. **44** With B, **[yo, k2tog]** 24 times, yo, k1. **45** With A, knit. **46** With A, yo, purl to last stitch on dpn, yo, k1. **47** With B, knit. **48** With B, yo, purl to last stitch on dpn, yo, k1. **49** With C, knit. **50** With C, yo, purl to last stitch on dpn, yo, k1. **51** With A, knit.

24

Shirley Paden

NEW YORK, NEW YORK

This swatch represents the knitting technique that was my first love — colorwork. It also represents spring which for me is always a time of joy. When you knit the entire afghan, it is my hope that your eyes will scan the beautiful squares and as you see this one your heart will be warmed with thoughts of sunshine and bloom!

MC Silver
125 yds

A Greystone Heather
B Tibetan Rose
C Flamingo Pink
25 yds each

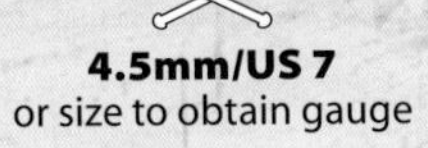

4.5mm/US 7
or size to obtain gauge

Notes 1 *See page 52 for unfamiliar abbreviations and techniques.* **2** *Shirley worked her square completely in intarsia. We suggest working the stems and tendrils in duplicate stitch.*

Square

With A, cast on 61. Knit 5 rows, end with a WS row. Keeping first and last 3 stitches in garter stitch (knit every row) with A, work center 55 stitches in Chart for 5 rows. ***Begin Short rows: Next row*** (WS) **[K3, wrap next purl stitch, turn, k3, turn, work in pattern across all stitches, hiding purl wrap.]** ***Next row*** (RS) **[K3, wrap next knit stitch, turn, k3, turn, work in pattern across all stitches, hiding knit wrap.]** Work 2 rows even through Row 70, ending last repeat. Work 3 rows even. Knit 5 rows with A. Bind off.

DUPLICATE STITCH

With a blunt tapestry needle threaded with a length of yarn of a contrasting color, cover a knitted stitch with an embroidered stitch of the same shape.

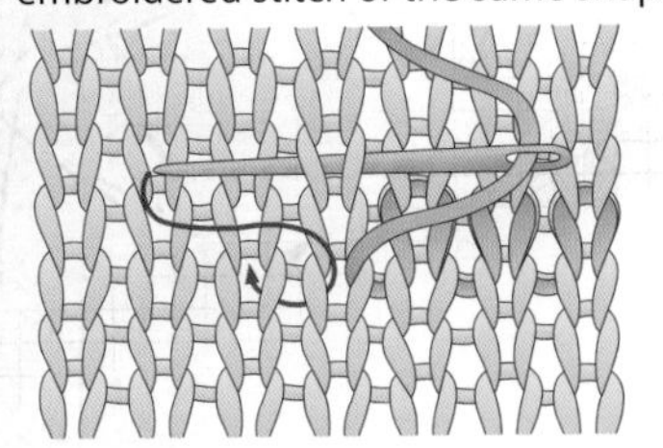

Short row wrap, knit side

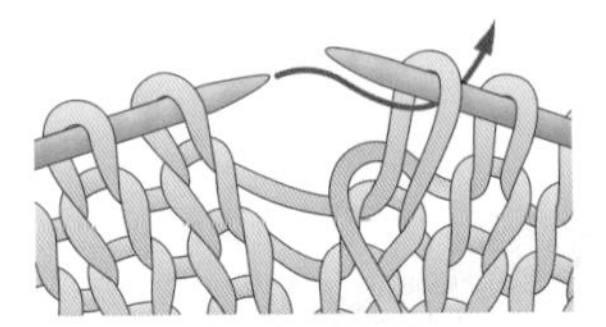

With yarn in back, slip next stitch as if to purl. Bring yarn to front of work and slip stitch back to left needle as shown. Turn work

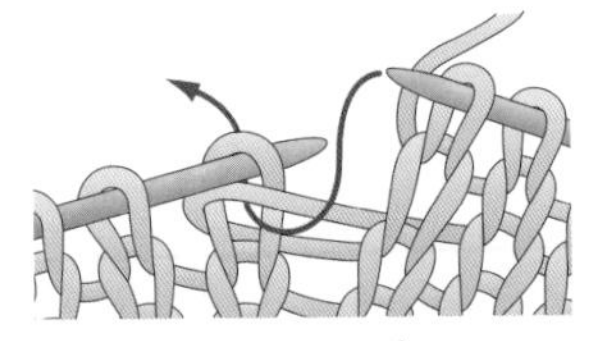

When you come to the wrap on a right-side row, make it less visible by working the wrap together with the stitch it wraps.

Purl side

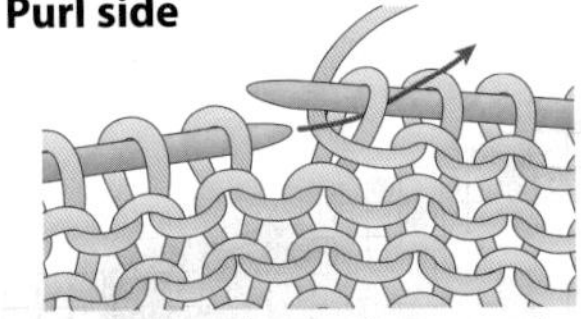

With yarn in front, slip next stitch as if to purl. Bring yarn to back of work and slip stitch back to left needle as shown. Turn work.

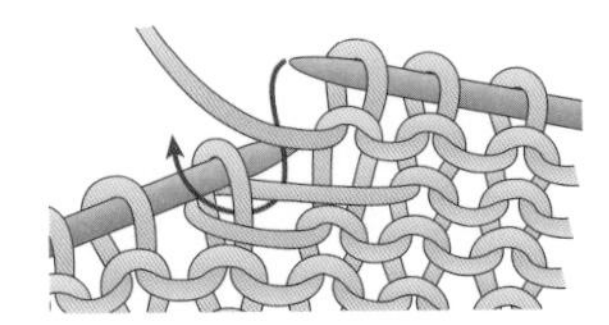

When you come to the wrap on the following purl row, make it less visible by inserting right needle under wrap as shown, placing the wrap on the left needle, and purling it together with the stitch it wraps.

70
60
50
40
30
20
10
1
55 stitches
Color Key
Silver (MC)
Greystone Heather (A)
Tibetan Rose(B)
Flamingo Pink (C)
Greystone Heather (A) duplicate stitch
Tibetan Rose (B) duplicate stitch

abbreviations

b in back of stitch
CC contrasting color
cn cable needle
cm centimeter(s)
dec decreas(e)(ed)(es)(ing)
dpn double pointed needle(s)
g gram(s)
" inch(es)
inc increas(e)(ed)(es)(ing)
k knit(ting)(s)(ted)
M1 make one
m meter(s)
MC main color
oz ounce(s)
p purl(ed)(ing)(s)
pm place marker
PSSO pass slipped stitch(es) over
RS right side(s)
sc single crochet
sl slip(ped)(ping)
SKP slip, knit, psso
SSK slip, slip, knit 2tog
st(s) stitch(es)
St st stockinette stitch
tbl through back of loop(s)
tog together
WS wrong side(s)
wyib with yarn in back
wyif with yarn in front
yd yard(s)
yo (2) yarn over (twice)

metrics

To convert the inches measurements used in our instructions to centimeters, simply multiply the inches by 2.5.
For example: 4" x 2.5 = 10cm

Charts and symbols

Our charts show the right side (RS) of the fabric. In general, each "square" is a stitch; a row of squares represents a row (or round) of stitches. Heavy lines on the charts are used to define pattern repeats.
RS. When facing the RS of the fabric, read the chart from right to left as you work and work the stitches as the symbols indicate. If you are working circularly, work every round thus.
WS. If you are working back and forth in rows, every other row will be a wrong side (WS) row. Read WS rows from left to right as you work.

Knitter's School

Loop cast-on

Often used to cast on a few stitches for a buttonhole. Loops can be formed over the index finger or thumb and can slant to the left or to the right. On the next row, work through back loop of right-slanting loops.

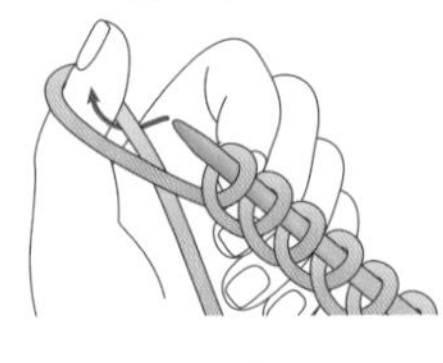

Left-slanting

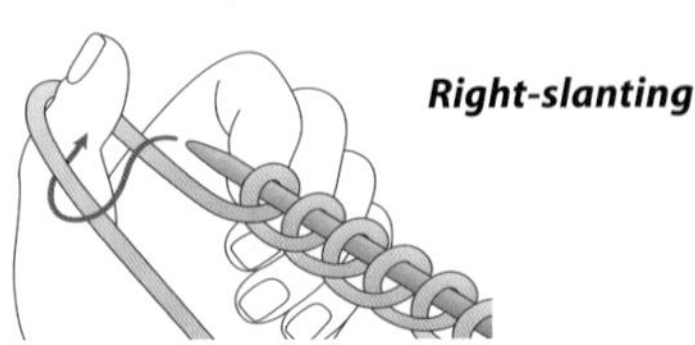

Right-slanting

3-needle bind-off

Uses. Instead of binding off shoulder sts and sewing them together.

Seam effect. Place *right* sides together, back stitches on one needle and front stitches on another. *K2tog (1 from front needle and 1 from back needle). Rep from* once. Bind first stitch off over 2nd stitch. Continue to k2tog (1 front stitch and 1 back stitch) and bind off across.
Ridge effect. Place *wrong* sides together, then work as above.

Stockinette graft

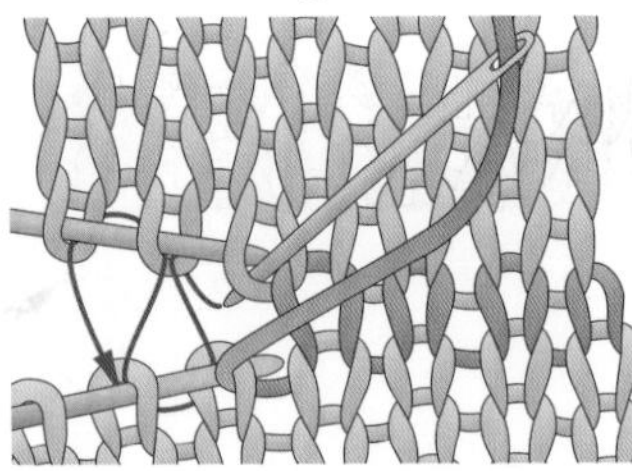

1. Arrange stitches on two needles.
2. Thread a blunt needle with matching yarn (approximately 1" per stitch).
3. Working from right to left, with right sides facing you, begin with preparatory steps 3a and 3b:
3a. Front needle: yarn through 1st loop as if to purl (from the back), leave stitch on needle.
3b. Back needle: yarn through 1st loop as if to knit (from the front), leave on.
4. Work 4a and 4b across:
4a. Front needle: through 1st stitch as if to knit, off needle: through next st as if to purl, leave on.
4b. Back needle: through 1st stitch as if to purl, off needle: through next st as if to knit, leave on.
5. Adjust tension to match rest of knitting.

Invisible cast-on

Uses. As a *temporary cast on*, when access to the bottom loops is needed.

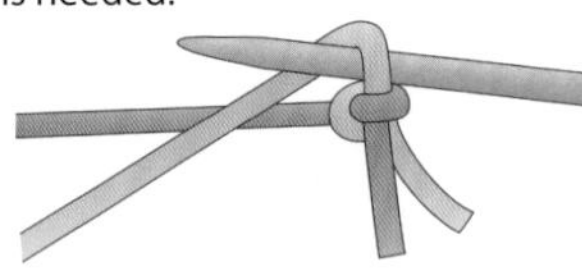

1. Knot working yarn to contrasting waste yarn. With needle in right hand, hold knot in right hand. Tension both strands in left hand; separate the strands with fingers of the left hand. Yarn over with working yarn in front of waste strand.

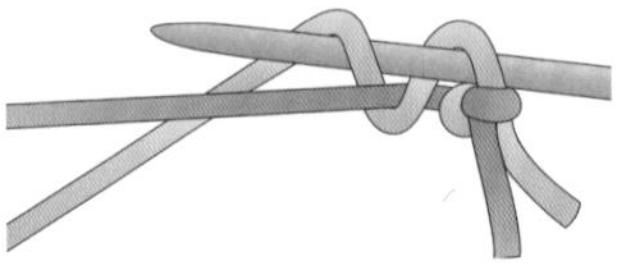

2. Holding waste strand taut, pivot yarns and yarn over with working yarn in back of waste strand.
3. Each yarn over forms a stitch. Alternate yarn over in front and in back of waste strand for required number of stitches. For an even number, twist working yarn around waste strand before knitting the first row.
4. Later, untie knot, remove waste strand, and arrange bottom loops on needle.

Intarsia

When changing from one color to the next when working intarsia, it is necessary to twist the yarns to prevent holes. Pick up the new color from under the old color, as shown, and continue working.

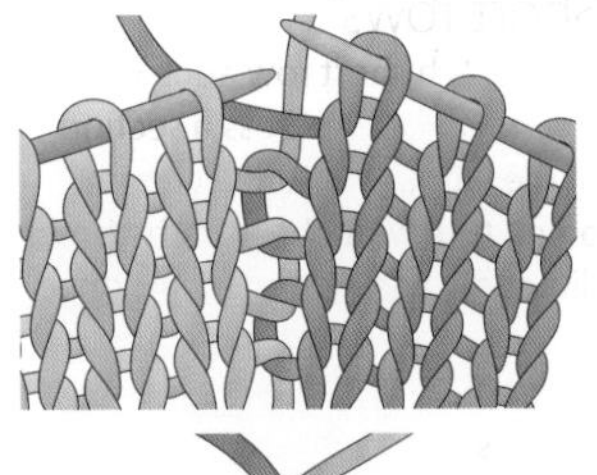

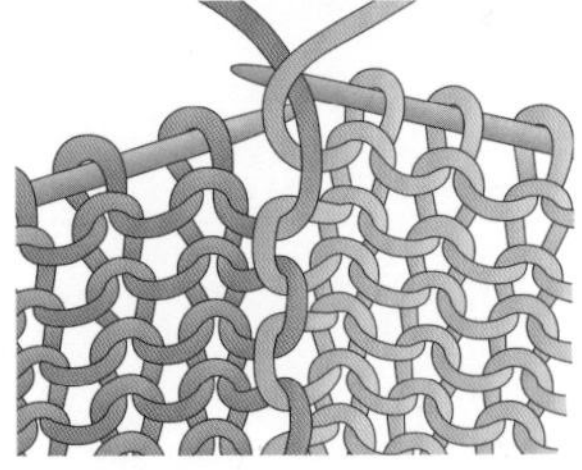

Duplicate stitch

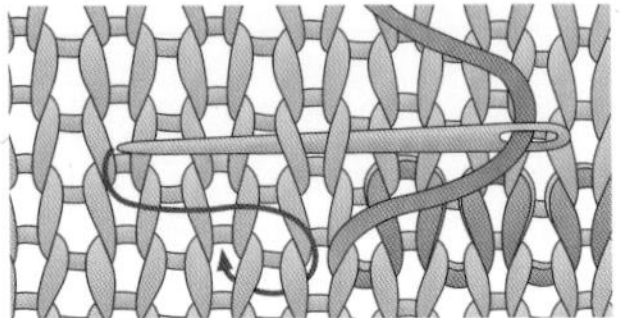

Duplicate stitch (also known as *swiss darning*) is just that: with a blunt tapestry needle threaded with a length of yarn of a con-trasting color, cover a knitted stitch with an embroidered stitch of the same shape.